TONIGHT in JUNGLELAND

ALSO BY PETER AMES CARLIN

*The Name of This Band Is R.E.M.:
A Biography*

*Sonic Boom: The Impossible Rise of Warner Bros. Records,
from Hendrix to Fleetwood Mac to Madonna to Prince*

Homeward Bound: The Life of Paul Simon

Bruce

Paul McCartney: A Life

*Catch a Wave: The Rise, Fall, and
Redemption of the Beach Boys' Brian Wilson*

TONIGHT in JUNGLELAND

Peter Ames Carlin

DOUBLEDAY
New York

FIRST DOUBLEDAY HARDCOVER EDITION 2025

Copyright © 2025 by Peter Ames Carlin

Penguin Random House values and supports copyright. Copyright fuels creativity, encourages diverse voices, promotes free speech, and creates a vibrant culture. Thank you for buying an authorized edition of this book and for complying with copyright laws by not reproducing, scanning, or distributing any part of it in any form without permission. You are supporting writers and allowing Penguin Random House to continue to publish books for every reader. Please note that no part of this book may be used or reproduced in any manner for the purpose of training artificial intelligence technologies or systems.

Published by Doubleday, a division of Penguin Random House LLC, 1745 Broadway, New York, NY 10019.

Doubleday and the portrayal of an anchor with a dolphin are registered trademarks of Penguin Random House LLC.

Grateful acknowledgment is made for permission to reprint previously published material on page 241.

Library of Congress Cataloging-in-Publication Data
Names: Carlin, Peter Ames, author.
Title: Tonight in Jungleland : the making of Born to Run / Peter Ames Carlin.
Description: First Doubleday hardcover edition. | New York : Doubleday, 2025. | Includes bibliographical references.
Identifiers: LCCN 2025001789 (print) | LCCN 2025001790 (ebook) | ISBN 9780385551533 (hardcover) | ISBN 9780385551540 (ebook)
Subjects: LCSH: Springsteen, Bruce. Born to run. | Rock music—1971–1980—History and criticism.
Classification: LCC ML420.S77 C37 2025 (print) | LCC ML420.S77 (ebook) | DDC 782.42166092—dc23/eng/20250122
LC record available at https://lccn.loc.gov/2025001789
LC ebook record available at https://lccn.loc.gov/2025001790

penguinrandomhouse.com | doubleday.com

Printed in the United States of America
1st Printing

The authorized representative in the EU for product safety and compliance is Penguin Random House Ireland, Morrison Chambers, 32 Nassau Street, Dublin D02 YH68, Ireland, https://eu-contact.penguin.ie.

Contents

Prologue   1

1. Watch the World Explode   3
2. Nashville   10
3. Lost in the Flood   23
4. I Know Where You Live   33
5. Carnival Weekend   43
6. Rock 'n' Roll Future   52
7. Growing Young with Rock and Roll   59
8. Walk with Me Out on the Wire   67
9. Welcome to E Street   75
10. The Poets Around Here Don't Write Nothing at All   87
11. Wings for Wheels   95
12. The E Street Dance   102
13. Magic in the Night   110
14. Like a Vision   116
15. All the Wonder It Brings   123

16. Scooter and the Big Man   129
17. It's Elephants, Baby!   138
18. And Then You Were the Psychopath   147
19. The Heist   154
20. Tonight in Jungleland   165
21. Kutztown   176
22. The Bottom Line   187
23. Flying by the Seat of My Pants   199
24. Backlash   209
25. The Other Thunder Road   218
    Epilogue   229

Acknowledgments   235
Bibliography   249

TONIGHT in JUNGLELAND

Prologue

A hot evening in late July 2024. My girlfriend and I were hosting a dinner party in our backyard, a small gang of writers, DJs, music fans. Holding court at the end of the table, playing with the dog, looking relaxed and happy, was the music journalist and Bruce Springsteen chronicler Charles R. Cross, known to all as Charley.

As the evening unwound Charley had plenty of stories to tell. After all, he had been writing about music since he was a kid at the University of Washington *Daily*, where I first read him in the 1970s when my professor dad would bring the campus paper home. Charley had gone on to edit the Seattle music newspaper *The Rocket*. He wrote several acclaimed biographies of musicians. And he'd created *Backstreets*, the magazine devoted to Bruce Springsteen's career.

It was one of those magical dinners that slips through the hours toward midnight. But we never got around to talking about the singular passion that bonded me and Charley: the work of Bruce Springsteen.

Then, after everyone had headed home, a small miracle happened. When he got to his car, Charley discovered that his cell phone had run out of juice. His car door wouldn't open without it, so he came back to my house, hoping to bum enough charge to get on the road. Delightful! Now that everyone else had gone, he and I could talk about *Born to Run* and what I was trying to do with this book. I knew he'd have ideas—no one was smarter than Charley about this stuff. It was already close to midnight, but he was brimming with enthusiasm and suggestions.

When his phone finally woke up and he was about to leave, Charley stopped for a moment and caught my eye. "This is what you really need to figure out," he said. Bruce's first two albums were amazing, he continued. *Greetings from Asbury Park, NJ* was a head-spinning debut; *The Wild, the Innocent and the E Street Shuffle* expanded on it in songwriting, arranging, and especially the sound. But both of those albums had flaws. A song or two that didn't work, some awkward performances, that sort of thing.

Born to Run, on the other hand, was . . . he shrugged. He knew he didn't need to finish his sentence. We both knew what *Born to Run* was.

"That's what you need to find out," he said. "What happened? What changed?" He paused. "How did it all get so great?"

He unplugged his phone, said his goodbyes, and left.

Charley died a week later.

His question became my mission. This book is for him.

How did it all get so great?

Chapter 1

Watch the World Explode

On a page in his notebook, the song was coming together. It was the fall of 1973 and Bruce Springsteen was in Asbury Park, watching the street racers in their souped-up cars orbiting the Ocean Avenue/Kingsley Street circuit on a Saturday night. The parade of muscular, lovingly detailed automobiles stirred something in him—the way the cars animated their owners' spirits. The candy shades of red, purple, and blue, the racing stripes and hand-painted eagles, the dazzling chrome and shimmering glass. And the power of their engines: the low rumble as they idled, the jet roar of takeoff. On the circuit the drivers moved slowly, steering wheels trembling in their hands, fully alive in their vehicles' power and beauty.

Like animals pacing in a black, dark cage, senses on overload . . . / They're gonna end this night in a senseless fight / And then watch the world explode.

Circling and revving, drifting slowly and then blasting off. Where were they going? It was an interesting question, just as compelling as where they came from and what brought them out into the night, to circle with their friends and rivals, to put it all on the line. One car had words running down its flank, a chain of cursive letters canted forward as if pulled by the finish line off in the distance. A dare, a philosophy, an explanation. Or maybe the title of a movie. Did he actually see it on a passing racer? Or did it simply pop into his head? Something that ought to be on a car, or maybe on his own tour van. Bruce wrote it in his notebook, in case he forgot it. He'd never forget it.

Born to run.

By the end of 1973 Bruce Springsteen was in a tough spot. His first album on Columbia Records, *Greetings from Asbury Park, NJ,* had been released that January. Critics and a small cadre of fans had loved it, and his second album, *The Wild, the Innocent and the E Street Shuffle,* released that November, won the same acclaim, but also the same weak sales. That hard fact, along with a shift in Columbia Records' upper management, meant that Bruce had fallen increasingly out of step with his record company. It was taking longer and longer for his manager, Mike Appel, to get his calls returned. Especially now that he was trying to figure out when they'd be getting the money they'd need to fund recording sessions for Bruce's next album. *We need to think about it, Mike,* he kept hearing from the executives.

When he finally got an answer in the early weeks of 1974 the news was frustrating, at best. Go make a single, they said. If it sounds like it could be on the radio we'll pay for the rest of the album. Appel tried to protest: Bruce isn't a singles act, he argued. It's all about albums, that's been the plan all along. But that hadn't worked, the executives said. So this is your chance. Go make a single.

Appel took the news to Bruce, who absorbed it, nodded, picked up his notebook. He had a new song that felt different from what they'd done before. Maybe that's what they should work on. He wasn't done with it yet, but the bones, and the essential feelings, were there.

The chords for the song, and the melody of the verses, found their shape nearly immediately. Focused on directness, if not simplicity, the central part of the tune revolved around three basic chords, the I-IV-V progression heard in so many rock songs: "Louie Louie," "Twist and Shout," the Beach Boys' "Don't Worry Baby," and at least a dozen of Chuck Berry's most classic hits, while the guitar riff in the verses combined "Telstar" with Duane Eddy's guitar twang. The descending chords in the second part of the verses, along with the I-vi-IV-V resolution of the chorus, traced their lineage to another corner of rock history (think "Duke of Earl," "This Boy," "Surfer Girl," et al.), while the ascending modulations in the bridge and the fast tumble back down to the root chord at the start of the next verse are the only traces of the elaborate constructions on Bruce's first two albums. The bones of this song came from rock 'n' roll's most fundamental musical archetypes.

One early draft of the lyrics was called "Wild Angels." Scrawled on a sheet of lined notebook paper, the verses describe a litany of modern urban catastrophes. Murderous junkies turn shotguns on soldiers on leave from Fort Dix. *Them wild boys did it just for the noise / Not even for the kicks.* Roads crumble, drivers are crushed beneath their own cars. The game is so rigged, it's murderous. *This town'll rip the bones from your back / It's a death trap / You're dead unless you get out when you're young.*

He wrote more drafts, filling notebook pages in hotel rooms in the wee hours after shows, or while lounging on the musty sofa in the little bungalow he'd recently rented in a working-class section of Long Branch, north of Asbury Park on the Jersey Shore. The lyrics evolved, but the darkness persisted. *Baby, tonight I saw the fast rebel / Crushed beneath the wheels of his own hemi* began one verse. By the end we see the rebel breathing his last, clutched in the arms of his "beautiful surfer girl." In another version the narrator witnesses the death of *all* his heroes, *crushed beneath the weight of / Their own Chevy Six.* And what of the beautiful surfer girl? . . . *Dead on a beach in an / Everlasting fix.*

It feels unexpected, nothing like the songs on his first two albums and even less like the work he'd do over the next few decades. But in the moment, as he was watching the world and absorbing the culture that reflected how it felt to be alive in that moment, it had the ring of truth. "I was naturally close to a sort of rock 'n' roll gothicness," he says. "That was just where I was coming from, from all the B movies I saw, and from growing up in Asbury Park with the hot rods, you know, spinning around the circuit on a nightly basis."

Bruce kept working, filling his notebook. Taking out lines, adding new ones, revising what he had, pulling it apart, crafting new verses and weaving those in. Eventually the words began to clarify and lose their hysterical edge. The gloom, and the sense of danger, persisted. Still, by the start of the spring Bruce's words identified something glimmering on the horizon. A vision, at least, of somewhere else. A potential end point for the one phrase that could be found in every draft of the lyric: *Tramps like us, baby we were born to run.*

It's the early fall of 2024, the morning of Bruce Springsteen's seventy-fifth birthday. We're in the living room of a house on the New Jersey shore a few miles south of the town Bruce's songs have made famous. It's a nice, if not extravagant, beach house, the sort of new construction that feels like it could have been here a century ago. But the enormous seaside windows and unexpected angles of the living room describe a more recent history. Sitting in an armchair that faces a large fireplace, Bruce is remembering what it was like to be a twenty-four-year-old kid. His dark eyes are sparkling. Just a week ago he played a weekend-capping show at the Sea.Hear.Now festival in Asbury Park. The festival's main stage was on the beach where the younger Bruce used to surf, swim, and, when he didn't have anywhere else to go, sleep. To mark the occasion he dispensed with the set list he'd built for the shows he'd been playing on tour over the last two years and dug deep into his earliest albums with rarely-played-these-days songs, including "Blinded by the Light," "Does This Bus Stop at 82nd Street?,"

"The E Street Shuffle," "4th of July, Asbury Park (Sandy)," and the 1973 outtake "Thundercrack." After the concert he threw a small after-party in the back room of the Wonder Bar, one of his oldest haunts in town. Refueling with a cheeseburger and fries, he exulted over the show and the sight of all those faces gazing up at him from the sand. "I kept thinking, this was the place, you know. This is where it all happened. Only there didn't used to be so many people here. It's coming alive, man. And it's great."

"Born to Run" came near the end of the show, in a ten-song run of bangers from Bruce's fifty-plus-year career that kept the crowd singing, dancing, and roaring. The scene would have been beyond his imagining when Bruce was trying to fulfill his record company's demand for a song that might appeal to more than his small cult of fans. But he'd already been a performing musician for close to a decade by then, and he knew what he could do when he set his mind to it. "You know, hey, it's a new day," he says. "It's a new world. It's a new life for me, and who am I? Let me decide on that, right? I'm not going to be defined by what other people are telling me, who I was or what I should be. I'm going to be defined by my own thoughts about who I am and who I want to be."

Who he wanted to be, what he hoped "Born to Run" would help him become, was this: a rock star.

Bruce introduced the song to the band at a rehearsal just after the start of January 1974. They were set up in the garage outside bassist Garry Tallent's father's place near Asbury Park. It was cold out there, the musicians wore sweaters, coats, and hats to ward off the chill, but the new song cut through the frosty air. Tallent clocked it immediately: "I just thought, 'Oh, that's a good one. That's a keeper, really.'" They ran through it a few times, Bruce explaining the song's pace and feel, slowing down to play the dozen or so changes in the bridge section. They set it aside for a week or so while they went up to Cambridge to play a three-night stand at Joe's Place, then put some more work into the new song during a quick stop at 914 Sound Studios in Blauvelt on their way back to New Jersey. "I think we had the song, or the bones of the song, and I was interested at first in getting the sound right," Bruce says, tossing a few logs onto the blaze he's got crackling in the expansive fireplace. "So we went up and recorded the song with very few lyrics. Maybe *tramps like us, we were born to run,* or maybe a few other things. Not a lot of the lyrics. But we started recording like that. And because we didn't really know how to get the sound we wanted it took us a long time."

While they were there Bruce showed them another new song, a sprawling, multisectioned piece called "Jungleland." This one was more complicated than the other tune, with more rough spots in the arrangement and some instrumental transitions Bruce hadn't started to figure out. He turned to his musically erudite pianist David Sancious for help, and they sketched a jazzy, piano-led vignette with the driving rhythm of "Kitty's Back," a recent tune that was the jazziest song he'd ever committed to vinyl. The lyrics were just as grim, if rudimentary, as those of the other new song, describing an evening under the pier with Fast Eddie and Cool Jerk, *gettin' hard and drinkin' beer* until the boardwalk rats turn their rage onto the narrator, lighting his shirt on fire and sending him reeling for home. Things were rough all over in Bruce's vision, where every evening ended in violence or some form of humiliation.

You throw up on your landlord's step / And you get up and go to work . . .

It was a strange and gloomy world, almost cartoonish in its violence and degradations. It was, in some part, a reflection of the diminished society Bruce saw through the windshield during those long drives on tour from city to city. The nation that had marched so boldly into the 1960s had wound up spending the decade being traumatized by assassinations, trapped in an unwinnable war, and tangled in racist myths that were as ancient and misguided as any fairy tale. The first half of the 1970s had been even more dispiriting, with the long, slow reveal of President

Nixon's criminality, an unwinding economy, and spiraling inflation caused in part by the Arab oil embargo. This also resulted in gas shortages that struck at America's most essential ideas about itself: independence, self-determination, and the freedom to hop in your car and go anywhere, anytime. The nation's horizons were closing in, its sense of possibility, and spirit, foreshortened. What had been a land of dreams had awakened in the withering light of an unforgiving dawn.

And Bruce's own sense of possibility, at least when it came to his career as a recording artist, was also beginning to fracture.

Chapter 2

Nashville

It was Monday morning, January 28, 1974, somewhere between Norfolk and Nashville. Bruce, in faded jeans and a hooded sweatshirt worn over a T-shirt, slouched in the passenger seat of a rented station wagon. His guitars rode on the back seat, the other luggage in the way back. His songwriting notebook—eighty pages of lined paper, the kind high school students use in class—sat next to him on the front seat. Mike Appel drove while Bruce worked the radio dial, twisting from left to right and back again, searching the static for a good song.

The two made an unlikely but surprisingly well-matched pair. Appel was a few years older, with shorter hair, neater clothes, and the restless energy of a man who was trying to get somewhere else. Bruce was just as ambitious but moved through the world more quietly. He talked less, tended to the edges of the room, and kept watch. When something caught his eye he reached for his notebook and clicked open his pen. You never knew what he was seeing, what he was thinking, not until he stepped onto the stage, saw his musicians around him, and counted to four.

One song ended and the headlines crackled from the dashboard speakers. Another Nixon aide had pleaded guilty to conspiring in the Watergate scandal. Muhammad Ali and Joe Frazier were preparing for their latest rematch. Bob Dylan's tour with the Band was about to play three concerts at Madison Square Garden, Dylan's first advertised show in New York in nearly a decade. Another piece of news caught Bruce and Appel's ear: the Arab oil embargo was squeezing the gas supply and sending prices rocketing to fifty cents a gallon and beyond. The nation's gasoline reserves were dwindling, and Congress was warning citizens to gird for rationing. Bruce wondered how they were going to get from show to show without gas for their cars. Appel said it was for him to worry about; Bruce should focus on the songs. Bruce reached over, picked up his notebook, held it on his lap, felt for the pen in his pocket. It was one of the few things he always had with him: pen and paper, guitars and cords, strings, picks, a few pairs of socks and underpants, T-shirts and sneakers. Everything he needed to survive in the world he'd made for himself, on the highway, perpetually on the move, chasing his vision.

Some days were easier than others. But even at its worst it was, for Bruce, the realization of the life he'd set out to have since he was fourteen years old.

"We're on the road. We're touring, even though the conditions are not good," he remembers. "I'm only twenty-four years old, so hey, how bad can it be for a twenty-four-year-old kid?" Maybe everything makes sense when you see it from fifty years in the future, with the beach just outside and a fire crackling in front of you. But back then spending a morning in front of a fireplace just a few minutes from his hometown would have felt like a waste of time. "I'm young, I'm traveling around the United States, and my life's dream is funkily coming true, you know."

This January day was all grind. Ten hours to Nashville, with Bruce and Appel in one rented station wagon and the five-member band in another, while their instruments, amplifiers, and other gear traveled in a van with their two roadies. It helped that they were coming off a successful pair of shows in Virginia. They started the weekend in Richmond, drawing a sellout crowd of 3,400 to the Mosque, an old-fashioned theater at Virginia Commonwealth University, on Friday the twenty-fifth, and continued to Norfolk the next night, playing for a near-capacity throng of 2,000 at the Chrysler Hall. The cash they took away from the back-to-back shows would keep them going for a month.

Going was what they did best. Driving through the day to get to a show, then driving through the night to get to another. Appel wasn't always with Bruce and the band; he had work to do back at his office in New York. But he came out for this run in early 1974 and so here they were together, the manager behind the wheel, his client riding alongside or stretching out in the back seat. Late one night they were on an empty highway, the headlights punching through the blackness. Nighttime was when Bruce was most awake, wheels spinning, leaning over the front seat, talking about the next album he wanted to make. How it should be different from his two previous albums. How he could hone his style to make his songs sleeker, faster, and more powerful. Like the singles Phil Spector made in the early 1960s, or like the songs that came out of the Brill Building in its glory days. Jeff Barry and Ellie Greenwich, Carole King and Gerry Goffin. Songs that were straightforward but full of feeling. That hit you in the gut and made you feel something so powerful you didn't notice how much it was making you think.

Pop songwriting was a subject Appel knew something about. He'd started writing songs when he was a teenager, crafting tunes to play with his high school band. He'd stuck with it for a few years and had enough success that when he gave up performing he quickly landed a job as a contract writer for song publishers. A few years later he and his writing partner, Jim Cretecos, set out to become managers and producers, and had signed an act or two by the fall of 1971 when a mutual friend introduced them to this talented kid from the Jersey Shore. That changed everything for them all. Appel and Cretecos left their songwriting jobs while Bruce put his music and, thus, his life in their hands. He was particularly close to Appel and trusted him so implicitly he barely read the management and publishing contracts his new manager had given him to sign. From that point forward Bruce had an advocate, a protector, and a record producer.

Appel also served as an editor as Bruce chose and honed the songs for his first two albums, and the musician had come to see his manager as a partner in his creative endeavors, something between a big brother and father figure as he worked to build a career in the recording industry. Now that the executives at Columbia had made it clear that his recording contract was on the line, Bruce wanted to make certain his new songs had the economy and drive to fit on the radio, even as they traced some of the shadier corners of modern American culture. In the dark of the wee hours, cruising down the highway, he could see it all. Bruce knew the songs on the first two albums were good; he could feel their impact when he and the band played them in the clubs night after night. But now he needed to reach beyond his existing audience and make music that would appeal to more listeners who weren't fans and hadn't seen him perform. First they needed to pass muster with radio programmers, and, before them, with the executives at Columbia Records. Achieving that would require a more direct, immediately accessible sound. But what did he need to do to get there? Appel had thoughts.

All those songs Bruce had mentioned, the Spector songs, the Greenwich/Barry songs, the King/Goffin songs, the manager observed, had lyrics that were conversational. Direct, first person, the singers describing their lives and feelings like they were talking to a friend. And because they were writing songs, they left plenty of space between the words so the melody came through. But Bruce's songs, like "Blinded by the Light," sounded like lyrical Gatling guns: words upon words upon words. "But you can't do that with a Phil Spector production," Appel said. "It's never gonna work. You gotta leave more room for melody." For example, Appel sang a few lines from one of Paul McCartney's most famous ballads: *The lonnnnnng and wiiiinnnnnding road . . .* bum-bum, bum-bum, *That leads* (pause) *. . . to your door . . .* See how much space he's leaving for the melody? Bruce thought about it, nodded, and said he got it. A few days later he showed Appel a new draft of lyrics for "Born to Run." A week or so after that he had another revision. Then another, and another. "He had five different versions of the 'Born to Run' lyrics," Appel says. "And finally I said to him, 'Don't ask me anymore which one I liked the best. I like all five versions. If you're gonna ask me again, I'm just gonna look at you and stare until you get the picture that you've gotta decide, not me.'"

The highway blurred, the landscape slid past, a patchwork of winter fields, small towns, and an exurban sprawl of muffler shops, Waffle Houses, off-brand grocery stores, and strip clubs. Bruce imagined the lives of the people they whizzed past. Sometimes he'd spot something that had him reaching for his notebook. He scribbled down what he saw, let it simmer in his imagination. He was looking for the kind of inspiration that had led him to write "Kitty's Back," a recent song spurred by a drive-by glimpse of a strip club whose marquee celebrated the return of a popular dancer. He and the band had been performing the song for months now, whipping up that frenzy where the whole room jumped and swung and shouted along: *Kitty's back in town, here she comes now / Kitty's back!*

The highway spoke to him, the beat-up cars and the hot rods, the guys standing on the corner with their hands in their pockets and a knowing gleam in their eyes. The bosses, the hitters, the hot-rodders, the down-and-outers hatching that sure thing, the one that was going to change everything. Bruce knew their struggle all too well.

They got to Nashville after dark, found their way to the Holiday Inn on Robertson Parkway, and settled in for the night. Or tried to, anyway. The hotel had been built next to the railroad, and the rooms Appel had procured for the group, the cheapest in the place, were at the rear of the building, hard on the tracks. The freight lines ran around the clock and when the trains rolled through they came like earthquakes. "Your whole room shook," Bruce recalls. "It was a memorable stay, which to this day I remember as being a bit of a nightmare."

The musicians slept in as best they could the next morning, but Appel was up and out early, working on the scheme that had prompted him to book this pair of midweek shows. The CBS Corporation, owners of Columbia Records, which released Bruce's records, was holding a convention for its sales force in Nashville. Bruce and his band hadn't been invited to play at the event and nobody had encouraged Appel, or any other manager, to set up their own showcase in town. But Appel had been in the business long enough to know that you never get ahead by not taking risks. So he found a club with an opening and got Bruce on the bill. That morning he located a copy shop, mimeographed invitations to the shows, stapled them to some of Bruce's best reviews, and took them to Roger Miller's King of the Road Motor Inn, the country-music-themed hotel the company had taken over for the convention. Maybe the choice of hotel, and Nashville being the epicenter of the country music industry, should have told him something about which end of the company's roster they'd be focused on over the next few days.

Appel knew the top executives in CBS's sales force had next to no interest in the client he'd been representing for nearly two years. But he'd dealt with skeptics before and knew one thing for sure: if someone doubted Bruce Springsteen's potential to become a star, all he had to do was get them to see a show. Because Bruce changed when he stepped onto the stage. Became something bigger than he was everywhere else in the world, than he was on his first two albums. When he was up there, a guitar in his hands and his band behind him, he could make even the most disinterested observers stop, listen, and reconsider everything they thought they knew.

But first Appel had to get the conventioneers into the club. When he got to the King of the Road he went to the front desk and, with the confidence of a man who had bigger things on his mind, told the clerk he needed to drop off some information for the CBS sales force. Appel never claimed to be associated with the company, but he also didn't say he wasn't, so if the clerk on the other side of the counter misread the manager's assurance for authority, he wasn't going to correct him. The fellow took the stack, said of course, sir. Appel nodded, thanked him very much, and left.

The Texas blues guitarist Freddie King was booked to play six nights at Muther's Music Emporium, a newly opened nightclub surrounded by auto parts stores and light industrial buildings on Hermitage Avenue. Booked to open the Tuesday and Wednesday night shows, Bruce and the band knew they'd be making less than they'd grown accustomed to earning, and almost certainly be playing to smaller, less-focused crowds. But Appel had worked it so they got to play a complete ninety-minute set both nights, guaranteeing the CBS executives who showed up would get a full dose of what Bruce could do onstage.

Then it was showtime. The music playing over the club's system faded, then went silent, and the manager's voice came up. *Welcome to Muther's, we've got Freddie King, Nashville's favorite bluesman . . . but first let's hear it for Columbia recording artist Bruce Springsteen and his band!* Scattered applause, led by Appel at the soundboard and a small clutch of what seemed to be fans standing in a knot on the near-empty dance floor. The musicians stepped onto the stage, took up their instruments; Bruce strapped on his Telecaster, strummed, fiddled with a knob, heard the other guys waking up their instruments, a string getting twisted into tune. An instant later Bruce stepped to the microphone, heard his voice—"Testing, one-two"—in his monitor; turned to his bandmates; barked, "All right!"; and ripped into the opening chords of "Does This Bus Stop at 82nd Street?" The guitar jangling for four beats, a high hanging note from the organ, then a blare of saxophone from the newest band member, Clarence Clemons, as Bruce, off-mic, counted in the verse: *One! Two! One-two-three-four!*, and they were all in, full-tilt from the jump, sax blaring, drums smashing and crashing, organ pumping and piano going smooth and dense, Bruce's guitar the sound of neon shimmering across chrome.

Hey bus driver, keep the change / Bless your children, give them names / Don't you trust men who walk with canes / Drink this and you'll grow wings on your feet!

What had been a loping folk tune on Bruce's first album, piano and acoustic guitar up front, bass and drums thrumming gently in the background, had evolved into a fast, lean rock song, less a bus rumbling up the avenue than the A train thundering uptown on the express line. Four minutes later it pulled into the station, wheels screeching, sparks flying. Bruce said a quick *thankyouverymuch* and swung into a playful funk-jazz cover of Rufus Thomas's "Walking the Dog," stretched to nearly nine minutes on extended solos from the blond-tressed organist Danny Federici, pianist Sancious, and Clarence Clemons, the strikingly large saxophonist, and a slow-building guitar break from Bruce. Then came a pointed introduction, aimed at the CBS executives he assumed were in the room: "This next one is a song from our second album, which you can't find *anywhere* in town." He laughed, shook his head. "It's out there *somewhere*," he said, and launched the first-ever live rendition of "Incident on 57th Street," the ambitious reworking of *Romeo and Juliet* that leads off the second side of *The Wild, the Innocent and the E Street Shuffle*, the album that had been released just a couple of months earlier.

The band, six pieces including Bruce, stretched out even further on "Kitty's Back," whose middle section was built to accommodate extended solos, surging into the group chant of *Here she comes now, here she comes* and then the climactic *Kitty's back in town . . . Kitty's back!* From there, Bruce led his band into even deeper waters with the unreleased performance piece "Thundercrack," eleven-plus minutes of call-and-response vocals, dynamic shifts, and instrumental stops and starts. They took a quick break after that, then came back with a loose, jammy version of "You Mean So Much to Me," another romp dating back to the R & B–style outfit Bruce formed, and dubbed the Bruce Springsteen Band, in 1971. Next came a pair of songs from Bruce's first album, most notably a funked-up eleven-minute jam built around the first single, "Blinded by the Light," featuring more long solos and hyperactive drumming from Vini Lopez. The show sprinted to a sweaty, ecstatic conclusion with a wild version of "Rosalita," which was a crowd favorite even before it became a highlight of *The Wild, the Innocent and the E Street Shuffle*. Now the entire crowd was on its feet, whistling and cheering as loudly as they could, which would have sounded even more impressive if they had numbered more than three dozen.

And none of them, as it turned out, had come from the CBS convention. What Appel hadn't figured on was how rigidly structured the sales team's schedule would be, how deeply focused on country music the entire event was, with evening field trips to the Ryman Auditorium and to Johnny Cash's home, where the salesmen were each greeted personally by the country superstar. The odds that any of the sales executives could have detached themselves from the convention to attend an outside show, even if they wanted to go, were exceedingly slim. And smaller still were the odds that they would have gone that far for an artist whose first two albums had sold a combined forty thousand copies at a time when even a cult act like Fleetwood Mac, in its early iteration as an arty blues band, routinely sold more than two hundred thousand albums to its followers.

They played another set to a near-empty Muther's the next night, then packed up their gear and hit the road again, five-hundred-plus miles north through northern Tennessee into Kentucky, then on to Ohio and up to Cleveland to open for the British hard rock band Wishbone Ash in front of a capacity crowd at the 2,500-seat Allen Theatre. Booked to play a college in Springfield, Massachusetts, the next night, the band and their two-man crew left Cleveland just after midnight, driving east into a snowstorm that slowed traffic to a crawl and turned what would ordinarily have been an eight-hour journey into a hair-raising eleven-hour marathon. They arrived safely and got set up at the Springfield College cafeteria only to realize that the storm had grown into a full-on blizzard. The clouds dumped enough snow on the city that day to close the roads, meaning the vast majority of ticket holders wouldn't be able to get to the venue. When showtime arrived the band took the stage, saw something like thirty hardy, snow-tested fans looking back at them, and cracked up. Were they still going to play? Of course they were, and every bit as long and hard as they would to 3,000 people. They rocked hard for an hour or so, and when the blizzard caused the hall to lose power, Bruce found his way through the blackness to the piano and performed solo until the lights came back on, at which point the band returned and they finished the set.

Onward. They laid low until the streets were clear enough to get out of town, then headed south for a night or two at home on the Jersey Shore, then continued south to Atlanta to play three shows opening for NRBQ at Richards nightclub on February 7, 8, and 9. From there they had a day to rest before heading north again to Lexington, Kentucky, for one show on February 12, headlining in the student center at the University of Kentucky. They opened that set with "New York City Serenade," the sprawling portrait of the city at night, which began with a free-form piano piece by Sancious, a classically trained pianist who wove strands of Mozart and Thelonious Monk into his impressionistic tour of the urban demimonde. It was a challenging opener for a rock show, but the audience listened in a hush, then cheered wildly at its conclusion. Grinning happily after that, Bruce launched into a set heavy on *The Wild, the Innocent* songs, playing most of the album, along with "Walking the Dog," "Let the Four Winds Blow," and the extended arrangements of "Blinded by the Light" and "Does This Bus Stop." As always, they played fast and wild, with plenty of solos. "David Sancious could probably outplay ninety-five percent of the keyboardists in the United States," Bruce says now. "And the rest of the band was great, too. Yeah, Danny was a hell of an improviser. I could play the guitar, Clarence could play the sax. And we did a lot of music, you know. I would count the tempos off fast, and Vin would make sure they got a little bit faster. So by the time we got up to speed, we were just wailing through those songs. Like near punk level."

That made them a tough band to explain. A Dylan-esque singer-songwriter fronting a rock band that played rhythm & blues and jazz with the velocity of punk rock? Umm . . . It was no wonder record company salesmen, radio programmers, and concertgoers had no idea how to describe, let alone sell, Bruce Springsteen, his music, and his band.

The hall at the University of Kentucky was only half full, but as the student newspaper reported two days later, the students who showed up had been ecstatic. "Our records don't sell that well and sometimes we're lucky to play in front of 100 people," Bruce told Joel Zakem, the reporter from the student newspaper, in a backstage hallway just after the show. "But it's really fun to play in front of an audience like the one tonight."

If it was a particularly good show, it was also the last time Bruce would perform with all of the original members of his band. He'd have to replace half of his musicians within six months.

Photograph © Peter Cunningham

Chapter 3

Lost in the Flood

A year earlier things seemed so much more promising. Bruce had been brought into Columbia by the storied record producer and artists & repertoire executive John Hammond, whose previous discoveries included Benny Goodman, Billie Holiday, and Bob Dylan. Upon his arrival, Bruce was anointed by company president Clive Davis, who instructed his employees to give his new signing every possible advantage.

Some of the other Columbia executives heard it too. Ron Oberman was in the middle of his first day as a junior publicist in the spring of 1972 when John Hammond walked into his office, introduced himself, and started talking about this impressive new singer-songwriter he'd just signed. The kid was playing a solo show that night in the city, and Oberman should come, Hammond said. Oberman, who had worked as a music critic before jumping into publicity and was very aware of his senior colleague's track record as a talent spotter, made a point of going to the show.

He brought a friend, the *Rolling Stone* writer Paul Nelson, and when the lights went down they realized they were the only people in the audience. No matter, Bruce came out on time, took in the mostly empty hall, and, without even a glimmer of disappointment, started to play. It was just Bruce, his guitar, and songs they were hearing for the first time, but Oberman was knocked sideways by the performer's charisma: his focus on the lyrics, the intensity of his guitar playing. It was, he recalls, impossible to look away. After the show he went back to the dressing room and introduced himself: *I'm going to be your publicist,* he told Bruce, who seemed thrilled. It was the first time he'd ever spoken to a publicist, let alone one charged with making *him* famous. "We hit it off right away," Oberman says.

Al Teller, in Columbia's marketing department, was another early convert. Teller got an acetate disc of *Greetings,* put it on his office turntable, and dropped the needle. He received these advance pressings of Columbia product on a near-daily basis and made a point of listening to everything that came his way at least once. If something caught his ear, he might look up from his work. If he really enjoyed something he'd spin it again. But *Greetings* hit him harder than that. He put down the papers he was reading and focused on what he was hearing, song after song.

When the last notes of "It's Hard to Be a Saint in the City" faded he walked down the corridor and gathered up some of his colleagues so they could hear the album too. When that playing ended he prowled in another direction, dragged out a few others, and pulled them into his office for another spin. Acetate discs were fragile; they could only withstand ten or twelve plays before they wore out, and by the end of the day Teller had worn his advance down to a nub. "I went home thinking, *Who* is *this guy? I know this will never get on the radio, so how do I market this?"*

Ron McCarrell had his conversion at the Kenny's Castaways nightclub in the fall of 1972. Paul Rappaport, a junior executive with marketing, was a Dylan fan who came into *Greetings* expecting to be disappointed and came away enthralled. Michael Pillot, a regional publicist working out of New Orleans, then Houston, had the same experience. Peter Philbin, a Los Angeles writer who followed Bruce back to New York after seeing him at the Troubadour, was a fan before he scored a job in Columbia's publicity department.

Steadily Bruce's name, and the sound of his music, began to spread around the Columbia executive floors. Oberman, Rappaport, Teller, and Philbin stoked the fire in New York, Pillot built an outpost in the Southeast. Just a few guys in an immense corporation, but in an industry that runs on subjective judgments, where every attempt to apply an objective measure to predict what will connect with record buyers had failed, the individual passions of staffers were not just influential but crucial as the executives attempted to mete out the company's financial and institutional support among its artists. And for young executives like Rappaport and Pillot, who were still building reputations, fighting for an artist they believed in was a mark of a prescient music executive—unless they convinced the company to go all in on an artist who came to nothing, in which case it was the mark of someone who would soon be looking for a job somewhere else. But another measure of Bruce's magic was that his supporters were too impassioned to care.

"I can remember standing on a sofa and jumping up and down begging for money for live broadcasts," Rappaport says. "We had to be a squeaky wheel to get greased, so I was shouting, '*We're on the verge of rock 'n' roll history!*'"

Well, not quite yet. But Rappaport knew what he heard. And he wasn't wrong. And for at least the first year of Bruce's time on Columbia the president of the company agreed with him.

In the spring of 1972 Clive Davis had liked the demos Hammond helped produce for his new find, and when Bruce came up to meet with him a few days later, the label president heard him play another song or two in his office and was so impressed he signed him up on the spot. He also heard the future in Bruce's songs, and from that point they would let the young artist do virtually everything his way. Hammond pushed for Bruce to work in an unadorned folk music style, but Davis sided with Bruce's desire to record more songs with a band. When Bruce wanted to use a vintage postcard as the central image on the cover, Columbia's chief designer, John Berg, suspended his own strict rule of putting only artist portraits on debut albums and created a complicated package with the postcard-shaped panel hinged to the front cover. The company bought ads celebrating the new album in a variety of high-profile outlets, including the cover of *Billboard.* When *Greetings from Asbury Park, NJ* was released on January 5, 1973, Davis proclaimed Bruce the face of the company's future. The executive filmed a testimonial video for the company's salesmen to show to record store owners, reciting the periphrastic lyrics of "Blinded by the Light," the album's lead single. It was an awkward image but the balding, be-suited Davis was determined to illustrate his point that Bruce Springsteen "puts more images, thoughts, and ideas in one song than most artists put into an entire album."

Advance copies of the album mailed to critics were packaged with hand-signed letters from Davis urging them to listen and then to call him at his desk to discuss what they'd heard. It's unclear how many journalists took Davis up on his offer, but most of the reviews they published echoed and even amplified his belief in his new artist. Writing in *Creem,* Robert Christgau compared Bruce to Bob Dylan—a comparison that would come to bedevil the younger musician. In *Rolling Stone* Lester Bangs called the debut album "bracing as hell," concluding that Bruce was "a bold new talent with more than a mouthful to say." Big praise from serious critics writing in the most influential magazines.

When the album and its lead single, "Blinded by the Light," failed to capture public attention during their first two months on the market, Davis instructed his promotions executives to redouble their efforts, and the message went out across the company. "I'm sure you all know how important it is for us to exert a major effort in busting both the single and album by this artist," promotions executive Sal Ingeme wrote to his team in a March 13 memo. Whatever they did in response, it didn't work. Radio programmers continued to ignore "Blinded by the Light." The second featured single, "Spirit in the Night," also failed to connect with radio. The good reviews had done nothing to spur radio play—the hyper-wordy lyrics that Davis was so proud of, along with Bruce's rough-hewn voice, made him a tough fit on all but the most free-form stations—and sales tanked. At a point when it wasn't uncommon for moderately popular artists to sell records in the hundreds of thousands, sales of *Greetings* stalled somewhere around 20,000.

No matter; Bruce continued to receive the company's support. When the pop-jazz band Chicago, one of Columbia's hottest acts, made plans for a summer tour of sports arenas, the band invited Bruce to serve as their opening act. It was a significant break, gaining him nightly access to one of the moment's biggest audiences. Bruce's leg of the tour began on May 30 at the Cumberland County Memorial Arena in Fayetteville, North Carolina, and went on from there, with each night's crowd numbering in the tens of thousands, twenty to thirty times the size of the audiences Bruce was accustomed to facing. Other artists might have been thrilled to play such big rooms but Bruce felt out of his element. After a week he told Appel he wanted out: he couldn't abide playing for audiences that had no interest in him, and he didn't feel like he could ever win them over from the far side of a cold, echoey basketball arena. They played a pair of shows at Madison Square Garden, one of the nation's most prestigious big-league venues for rock bands, in New York on June 14 and 15, then jumped in their rented van and station wagons and bolted for the Jersey Shore.

Ditching the Chicago tour did nothing to endear Bruce to the Columbia Records executives. His stock fell even lower when Clive Davis was abruptly fired. The company's reasoning had no apparent ties to Davis's job performance—it revolved around what Columbia described as improper expense claims. Meanwhile, a federal investigation of the company looked into possible high-level ties to mobsters, payola, and drug distribution. The darker allegations never led to charges against Davis, and the exiled executive soon resumed his career as the founder of Arista Records. But the mid-1973 reshuffling of authority and priorities at Columbia had an immediate impact on Bruce's prospects. In attempts to stabilize its dominant record label, the CBS corporate leadership brought in Irwin Segelstein, an executive with a long track record at CBS Television, to fill Davis's role. Admittedly more expert in corporate administration than popular music, Segelstein empowered artists & repertoire executive Charles Koppelman, telling him to use his judgment on musical matters. Koppelman hadn't been involved with Bruce's signing or development, so he had no allegiance to him or any investment in his career. And he was still getting acquainted with his new job when the gloomy sales statistics for *Greetings* were darkened by Bruce's one-two summertime punch of abandoning the high-profile Chicago tour and then making what appeared to be a purposefully unimpressive appearance at CBS's sales convention in San Francisco at the end of that same July.

Bruce, meanwhile, paid attention to what he could control: playing shows and writing new songs. If you saw Bruce offstage, at home, or on the road in 1973 and 1974, you wouldn't have to look very far to find his songwriting notebook. He usually kept it within reach and always had a song, or more likely several songs, working at the same time. Chords, notes on feel, and lyrics. The band got used to having him show up at rehearsals with new material for them to learn; virtually all of their sets included new or unrecorded songs. "Thundercrack" and "Rosalita (Come Out Tonight)," both written to be performance pieces with multiple stops, starts, and wild climaxes, quickly became crowd favorites. "Zero and Blind Terry" and "Secret to the Blues" also featured regularly at shows, as did the solo acoustic "Circus Song" and the mostly acoustic (with Federici on accordion) "4th of July, Asbury Park (Sandy)." "New York City Song" and "Kitty's Back" boasted significant contributions from David Sancious, who rejoined the band in May of 1973, taking on the piano while Danny Federici focused on organ.

In the late spring of 1973, with a critically acclaimed but commercially failed album and more than six months of nonstop stage work behind them, Bruce and the band returned to 914 Sound Studios in Blauvelt to turn the new material into a second album, recording in fits and starts between bookings through June, July, and August. They only had a handful of tracks recorded when Appel got a call from Koppelman, who said he wanted to hear what they had been working on. Appel compiled a tape of five tracks in progress, including another new rave-up, "Seaside Bar Song," and "The Fever," a sultry R & B–style love song, and took it to CBS headquarters in midtown Manhattan, where Appel and his assistant Bob Spitz sat with Koppelman and his A & R colleague Kip Cohen. Half an hour later Koppelman was distinctly unimpressed by what he'd heard. Bruce, he decreed, had a lot of work ahead of him. Maybe he wasn't ready to make a new album? Appel wasn't happy to hear it. He snapped and snarled and told Koppelman he was deaf, had no idea what he was hearing. But the executive just shrugged, offered some lukewarm encouragement, and sent them on their way.

Back in the studio Bruce revised "New York City Song" into the darkly poetic "New York City Serenade," working with Sancious to craft its elaborate piano intro, and with the entire band to turn the sprawling, jazz-inflected "Kitty's Back" into an instrumental tour de force, with each soloist contributing fiery performances. "Incident on 57th Street" was a rock 'n' roll *West Side Story*, giving the doomed romance of Spanish Johnny and Puerto Rican Jane the tragic grandeur of *Romeo and Juliet*. "The E Street Shuffle," meanwhile, described the Asbury bar scene in transcendent terms, the band and dancers coming together into one ecstatic, leaping mass. It became the title song, more or less, for the second album: *The Wild, the Innocent and the E Street Shuffle*. Released with the holiday rush in early November, the album received near-unanimous good reviews, next to no radio airplay, and an initial wave of sales that was only a slight improvement over what *Greetings* had done. More than anything it served as an illustration of how far Bruce's star had tumbled in the ten months since *Greetings* had emerged into the world and he had been declared the next Bob Dylan, a brilliant artist already on his way to being a superstar.

When he heard *The Wild, the Innocent and the E Street Shuffle* before its release in the late fall of 1973, John Hammond, the artists & repertoire executive, still thought Bruce sounded like Bob Dylan, the game-changing artist he'd signed in 1961. Only now the songs were clanging in his ears like Dylan's did once he traded his acoustic guitar for a Fender Stratocaster and hired a crew of louts to turn his brilliantly poetic folk songs into rock 'n' roll. Not that Hammond dismissed all rock, he wasn't as limited as that. But he knew how gifted a songwriter Bruce was. His compositions were so distinctive, Hammond believed, any attempt to add more instruments, voices, and effects was akin to sabotage. When he played the finished tracks of *The Wild, the Innocent and the E Street Shuffle* and heard all that production . . . the horns and funky clavinet on "The E Street Shuffle"; the extended guitar, organ, and sax solos on "Kitty's Back"; and the ecstatic rock 'n' roll of "Rosalita," all of it, he sighed and shook his head.

Many critics disagreed. "Another stone, howling, joyous monster of a record," Bruce Pollock wrote in *The New York Times*. "There's just no way that folks are going to be able to sidestep the raw beauty of 'New York City Serenade,' the heat of '4th of July, Asbury Park (Sandy),' or the infectious drive of 'Rosalita,'" decreed *Cashbox*. "Here's to Bruce Springsteen, Superstar." Hammond just didn't hear it the same way. And when he received a letter from a Texas radio programmer raving about the album, he wrote back promptly, in his courtly fashion, to tell her he did not share her enthusiasm. "[I] am terribly disappointed in the second album . . . I have the feeling of material being far too carefully worked over." Still, Hammond included a clip of the just-published *Times* review, "an unadulterated rave," so she didn't feel like he was telling her she was wrong, exactly. "It's all pretty embarrassing for Columbia, since most of us here have felt that this album doesn't do him justice and are waiting for what ought to be a major effort on his next album."

Though as Hammond knew, not everyone at Columbia was as eager as he was to hear Bruce's next work. The excellent reviews Bruce received for his debut album did nearly nothing to interest the radio programmers on either side of the dial (AM or FM), who served as the primary gatekeepers for the airwaves and thus the ears of potential record buyers. This was disappointing but wasn't a reason for Clive Davis to lose patience with an artist in whom he had made such a public declaration of faith. But Davis's firing, and the resulting reshuffle of the company's managers, left a void of original execs who'd elevated Bruce to such a lofty place among the artists on Columbia's roster. While Davis and John Hammond had been busy cultivating the career of Bruce Springsteen, Charles Koppelman had been working with Billy Joel, a similarly young singer-songwriter who also came from just outside New York City. Joel shared Bruce's working-class background and sensibility, but his muse ran in a more tuneful, and seemingly more commercial, direction. The company didn't have limitless money and staff to promote its up-and-coming artists, and if they had to choose between Springsteen and Joel, Koppelman already knew who had earned his support. In January 1974, when he directed his staff to make a list of low-selling artists they should drop from the label, one of the names on it was Bruce Springsteen.

Whether the list was intended to direct immediate action, or a suggestion for moves they might make at some point in the future, wasn't clear. But when publicist Ron Oberman, who had been helping marshal support for Bruce on the executive floors since the first time he saw him perform in the summer of 1972, heard that his favorite artist was on the drop list, he marched back to his office and wrote an impassioned letter to Koppelman urging him to change his mind. Oberman next sent copies to all the senior executives, including newly appointed label president Irwin

Segelstein. Whether it had any impact on Koppelman's actions is also unclear. They didn't sever the label's contract with Bruce and didn't notify his managers that their client was on the short list for dismissal. All Appel knew for certain was that when he called the company looking to discuss plans to start recording Bruce's third album, nobody would take his call or return his messages. And when Appel finally got through, the message he got was tentative at best. Tell Bruce to make that single, they said. If it sounds like it could get on the radio we'll move forward. So Bruce went back to his guitar, flipped his notebook open to his latest draft of lyrics, and worked on polishing that new song he had.

Chapter 4

I Know Where You Live

When he introduced the band members onstage at the club show in Nashville—the show that was supposed to be full of Columbia execs—Bruce made it into a joke. All the intros were overblown and silly, noting that the bassist, "the master of the low notes!," was the scion of a family with a long history in show business: "His mother was a Tallent, his father was a Tallent, his sister was a Tallent, his brother was a Tallent, his great-great-grandfather was a great, great Tallent, on the bass guitar, from Long Branch, New Jersey, Mr. Garry W. Tallent!" And so it went, jokes all around, from Danny Federici making the teenyboppers fall to their knees to David Sancious playing notes that belong in quotes. And it only got sillier right up until he got to the drummer, who, Bruce confided in a stagey whisper, they kept at the rear of the stage for a reason. "The reason is because he's so vicious. He was diagnosed on the national syndicated daytime television show with Dr. Joyce Brothers as a homicidic, schizophrenic, paranoiac Roman Catholic. And the only man I know who snorts beer through his left ear, weighing in at one hundred sixty-five pounds of stone ugliness, from Asbury Park, New Jersey, the Mad Dog, the Madman, watch out, girls, he hates to be alone . . . Vincent Lopez."

Just as he did every time Bruce made him the climactic feature in his big gag introductions, Lopez laughed along. You could hear him cackling when Bruce got to the part about "stone ugliness," but the jokes about the homicidal drummer were inspired by Lopez's real, and at times fearsome, temper. And the tension it was causing among the band members and their management wasn't the least bit funny.

When they started playing together Lopez was arguably the bandleader. He was already looking for a guitarist and talking to local surfboard designer / factory owner Tinker West about managing his new band when he glimpsed Bruce at the Upstage club in early 1969 and invited him to join. Bruce wrote the songs and served as the front man in the group they eventually called Steel Mill, but Lopez's energetic drumming, along with his strong high harmonies and surprisingly delicate performances on recorder, revealed a musicality that made *drummer* an incomplete description of his role. Lopez—a broad-shouldered six feet three inches who knew how to use his size to back down shifty club owners and other antagonists—served as Bruce's protector. Sometimes he had to be his own protector, when some alpha dude swaggered in determined to get into a little kick-ass with the biggest guy in the room. And it didn't take much to get Lopez's fists raised, and not just with barroom bullies. Spending virtually every day in the company of bandmates—when they weren't on the road Lopez shared a house with Clarence Clemons and Danny Federici—would wear down anyone's patience, particularly given the poverty-level wages that Appel couldn't always pay them. When the pressure rose Lopez was usually the first to erupt.

Meanwhile, their sound was changing. The addition of Sancious, a classically trained pianist who was a skilled improviser and fluent in nearly every style of music, gave the band a wide-ranging jazzy feel. Bruce wrote "Kitty's Back" to give his bandmates room to show off their chops, and the other songs began to stretch out, too. By early 1974 "Thundercrack" usually went on for ten or more minutes, as did old R & B covers like "Let the Four Winds Blow" and "Walking the Dog." "Blinded by the Light" spanned nearly eleven minutes in Nashville, with long guitar and sax solos, an array of tricky rhythmic shifts, and other instrumental pyrotechnics. Tempos sped up, everyone played as hard as they could, and Lopez went at his drums with the wild abandon of Keith Moon. Except Moon's genius was in how his thundering chaos stayed in perfect time. Lopez was like a pocket watch when he played straight, but the band's new somersaulting style didn't suit him. He'd go into orbit with the other guys and still be airborne when everyone else landed together on the next break. Which wouldn't have been an insurmountable problem if he weren't also creating other kinds of havoc offstage.

The breaking point came in February. Bruce and the band were in the studio in Blauvelt working on "Born to Run" when Mike Appel's younger brother Stephen, who had joined the organization as road manager, showed up with the musicians' salaries. He handed the money to Lopez to distribute, but when the drummer realized there was less money than they'd been expecting, his temper jumped into the red zone. Finding Stephen in the lounge outside the studio, he stalked up to him, swearing, and shoved the cash back into his hands. Did the drummer punch the young road manager or just push him a little too hard? Witnesses disagree, except for the part where Stephen landed flat on his back and Lopez dashed outside and vanished into a nearby patch of woods. Embarrassed and furious, Stephen tossed the money aside, got into his car, and roared off. Bruce had only glimpsed the action through the doorway but saw enough to understand that the time had come to make a change. A day or two later Bruce fired Lopez, the man who had initially invited Bruce to be the guitarist and songwriter in his new band—though the authority had shifted fairly quickly to Bruce. Either way, Lopez was the only drummer he'd worked with for the last five years.

Now drummer-less, Bruce had Appel scratch all the dates they had booked for February 1974 so they could find, hire, and train a new musician. The manager set out to do just that, but one club owner in South Jersey refused to cancel. He'd already sold all the tickets and providing refunds to his patrons was not an option. And he meant it. Carlo Rossi was not just connected to organized crime but was actually a member of a major crime family, which meant he would not tolerate being embarrassed by these pipsqueak rock 'n' rollers. Drummer or no, Rossi told him, they would play the fucking show. Either that or he'd make them regret it. "I know where you live," he breathed into the phone ominously.

As Appel learned when he talked to another club owner with connections in organized crime, Rossi didn't hesitate to use muscle to get what he wanted. Bruce also knew a thing or two about mobsters, and when Appel said it would probably be beneficial to all of their health to play the show, he didn't argue.

The shattered society Bruce described in the early drafts of "Born to Run," with its broken roads, deadly cars, murderous drug addicts, and lifeless surfer girls, began to come into focus as the winter of 1974 ground on. Looking around, it was hard to identify anyone he could trust. His longtime drummer had gone rogue; his record company had fired the chief executive who had been his greatest advocate and replaced him with a TV executive who didn't know Bruce's name and had empowered executives who were seemingly bent on ending his career. Bruce's romance with live-in girlfriend Diane Lozito had fallen to ruin. The one thing he could always control was his performances, where and when he played, and under what circumstances. But just now when he needed a couple of weeks to break in a new drummer, a club owner was threatening to kill him. Set against the national backdrop of corruption, inflation, and shrinking horizons, it all made too much sense.

Near the end of 1973, Bruce found a small house in the West End section of Long Branch to rent for himself, lugged his belongings the few miles up the shore, and settled in. Sitting on the bed with his guitar and his notebook, he set to revising his lyrics.

> *Hot day we sweat it out in the streets*
> *Of a runaway American dream*
> *At night we stop and tremble in the heat*
> *With murder in our dreams*

Bruce's aunt Dora had given him a battered old spinet piano years earlier and he'd carted it with him to his rental in Long Branch, where he started sketching song ideas on the instrument. He wasn't as fluent on the piano as he was on his guitar, but he knew his way around the keyboard. Bruce had been trying to play the piano in his aunt's house since he was so small he had to reach over his head to put his fingers on the ivories. He grew more proficient as he got bigger and came to like how the physical layout of the keys created different melodic and chordal possibilities than his guitar. He could create a cinematic sound even when he was playing by himself and was steering toward more emotional, sonically grandiose visions. As composed on the piano, a tale of young love gone bad could ring like the collapse of a city, or even society itself.

One soft, infested summer, Billy and Terry became lovers together . . .

First he called it "Hidin' on the River," then "Early Life" or "Virgin Summer." Different titles, different lyrics. But the ringing sound of the chords on the piano reminded him of church bells and he could play them for hours and sense the town crumbling beneath him.

> *Endless juke joints on Valentino Drag*
> *Watchin the hitters work the fun house*
> *Rippin' off the fags*
> *Empty nights exploding into crazy, senseless violence . . .*

Before he joined Bruce's band in the spring of 1973 David Sancious had been building a band in Richmond, Virginia, playing original jazz fusion with Ernest "Boom" Carter, a drummer he'd known since they were both kids in Belmar, south of Asbury Park. Carter was just as diverse a player as Sancious and, Sancious said, would be a great addition to the band. When Carter came up from Virginia he proved to be just as skilled and as easygoing as Sancious had promised. Better yet he was quick to learn the many tricks and wrinkles in Bruce's set, which was particularly fortunate given the short runway leading up to the uncancelable date at the Satellite Lounge in Cookstown, New Jersey.

Carter got up to Asbury as fast as he could, they took two or three days to run him through the set, and they played a solid show for the sellout crowd.

They then packed up their gear and split for Bryn Mawr for a three-night stand at the Main Point, one of their most reliable, friendliest halls. The band went south from there, first for two shows at Georgetown University in Washington, DC, on March 3, then down to a series of dates in Texas, where they had never appeared. Unsure of what they would find in such unexplored territory, the band learned a quick lesson about what could happen when your music got played on the radio. When they got to Houston, where the popular free-form station KLOL-FM had programmed cuts from both *Greetings* and *The Wild, the Innocent,* Bruce and the band played to sold-out crowds at the 450-seat Liberty Hall, a single opening show on March 7, then two shows a night for three straight evenings starting March 8. They met the same kind of enthusiasm a few days later in Austin, where KLBJ-FM had played Bruce's records so consistently that Columbia's regional publicist Michael Pillot convinced Appel to give the station a tape of "The Fever," a slow-burning R & B–style song Bruce had recorded but opted not to put on *Wild*. The unreleased song connected with listeners and the back-to-back shows at the 1,500-seat Armadillo World Headquarters were both sold out. Then they got to Dallas, where no radio stations featured Bruce's music, for an eight-show, four-night stand at Gertie's nightclub, and played to a mostly deserted room.

From there they continued west to Phoenix, another city they'd never visited, bracing for another night like the four they'd just endured in Dallas. But that's not what they found on March 24 when they got to the Celebrity Theatre, a circular venue where acts played in the round. Instead it was jammed with cheering fans. "This doesn't happen to us everywhere, so when it does we appreciate it," Bruce enthused after the show. "We don't get this kind of reception. I don't know what's goin' on down here."

What was going on was that Bruce's records were getting airtime on Phoenix's free-form radio station KDKB-FM. Listeners picked up on "Spirit in the Night" and "Rosalita" and started calling the station to hear them again and again. Noting the surge of airplay for the new artist, the promoter booked the show for the 2,650-seat Celebrity Theatre, taking a risk on a first-time visitor. And it paid off splendidly: the show sold out, the audience went berserk, and when it was over the promoter booked the band for two additional shows in the theater at the end of July.

At the end of March 1974, Bruce and the band had a rare ten-day break, then returned to the reliable circuit in the Northeast, hitting universities, nightclubs, and small theaters around New Jersey, Pennsylvania, New York, and Massachusetts, including a four-night stand at Charlie's Place in Cambridge, Massachusetts, in early April. The engagement called for two shows a night, early and late. When Bruce ducked outside to get a breath of air between shows on April 10 he paused for a few moments to read one of the clips the club owner had taped to the window to draw in customers. What caught his eye was a mostly good review of *The Wild, the Innocent and the E Street Shuffle* that had been published in *The Real Paper*, one of Boston's alternative weeklies.

The piece was by Jon Landau, a local critic best known for being the record reviews editor of and a regular contributor to *Rolling Stone*. When Landau, who was being dragged into the show by fellow rock critic Dave Marsh, saw Bruce reviewing his own review, he stepped up and started a conversation.

"What do you think of this?"

Bruce kept reading.

"It's pretty good," he said, looking over at Landau. "This guy's got something to say."

Landau smiled and introduced himself, Bruce shook his hand, and then Landau went inside and left it at that. For the moment, anyway. He found Bruce after the show and they sat down to chat. They traded telephone numbers, and the next morning Bruce rang him up. What did you mean, he wondered, when you said the album wasn't well produced? That started a conversation that went on for a couple of hours, maybe longer. "We just drifted all over the place and we agreed to talk some more," Landau recalls. "That was the beginning."

Chapter 5

Carnival Weekend

Even a week later Bruce's face lights up when he thinks about the Sea.Hear.Now show he played on the Asbury beach in mid-September 2024. He started the set with "Lonesome Day," a relatively recent song that hits all the marks for a good opener: it rocks, isn't too tricky or hard to sing, lets him limber up, gets the crowd singing along. When it was over he let the ovation fade, said his hellos, then said he'd written the next one on the beach about five hundred yards from where he was standing. He ripped into the opening riff of "Blinded by the Light" and he was back at the beginning. Back into the same set list he played in bar after bar, up and down the East Coast, past the smelters and factories of the industrial Midwest, south to the fringe of Dixie, west to Texas, venturing to Arizona, then back east again. No matter where, no matter the size of the hall, jammed or empty. He'd throw himself into it like he was hurling his body against a brick wall. "Spirit in the Night," "Does This Bus Stop at 82nd Street?," "Thundercrack," "Growin' Up," "The E Street Shuffle." The crowd, 35,000 strong and out of their fucking minds with joy, were with him from the first note. And of course he loved it, but you know what else he loved? The days when nobody knew and nobody cared, when he could see the looks on their faces and watch the conversions happen, one by one, right in front of him. Some nights were better than others. But even when it was bad, as long as he was onstage he was having a blast.

"I hadn't had any real success, so I didn't know what I was missing," Bruce says. It's a cool morning and he's got that fire going, tossing logs onto the hearth, watching the flames flicker, jump, and dance. Every hour or so he gets up to get more wood and comes back with another huge armload. No, he doesn't want a hand. Makes a face if you ask to help. He's good, man, thanks. "All I know is, hey, I'm on the road. I got a great band. We're having the time of our lives. I'm not working nine to five, and I'm traveling around, staying in places that are nicer than my apartment. I'm living pretty good. I liked all the guys in the band and we're having fun. We're meeting girls. I mean, my recollection of all those times now are just good times."

Bruce's fire is roaring now; you can feel the heat on your face even from thirty feet away. "You know, I felt like I was as good as anybody out there," he says. "I felt we should make some impact, but I was just taking it a day at a time." The smoke is sweet and earthy, little pockets of sap boiling, sizzling, then exploding, small showers of sparks that go up like miniature fireworks.

The band arrived at Brown University on April 26, 1974. It was a Friday, the start of the weekend of the school's spring carnival, a party weekend with live music scheduled at different venues on campus throughout the day. The evening at Brown's Alumnae Hall began with an 8 p.m. show by the jazz pianist McCoy Tyner. When that performance ended the student workers cleared the hall and reset the stage, then let in the next crowd for the midnight show. Tickets were cheap, maybe $2.50 a head, and there was a just-okay crowd for a midnight show, maybe five hundred kids in a hall that could fit close to a thousand audience members. But the people who did come were very up to hear some rock 'n' roll, even if they weren't familiar with Bruce or his records.

And then there was John Garrett Andrews, who knew all about Bruce. He was a few years younger but had grown up near Bruce in Monmouth County in the 1960s and first saw the ambitious young guitarist perform with his high school band, the Castiles, in early 1968. Andrews also played in a teenage band back then and had been impressed enough by the Castiles to note Bruce's moves around the shore over the next few years. Now Andrews was studying at Brown and writing for the school newspaper. He figured he'd use his position to give his old neighbor a little boost in his corner of the Ivy League. Andrews pitched a profile to his editor, then set up an interview, slated to take place just after the show.

James Segelstein, on the other hand, only came because his friends wanted to go. His expectations for the evening were not what you'd call high. He was sick with mononucleosis, for one thing, so he made sure to go up to the balcony where there were seats, because he didn't have the energy to stand for an entire concert. His lack of enthusiasm wasn't because he didn't know Bruce's music. On the contrary, he'd heard his albums and didn't care for them. "My dad brought home the first two albums," he says. "I listened to them with my girlfriend at the time, and the two of us were thinking it was this really pathetic Dylan-esque thing. We were literally laughing while we sang: *Oooh, throwin' up . . .*"

Then the concert began. First came a hushed "New York City Serenade," with Sancious's dramatic piano introduction. The rest of the band came onstage, Bruce traded his acoustic guitar for his Telecaster and made a quick count-off, and they all went into a rambunctious take on "Spirit in the Night." Sitting in the front row of the balcony, his brow moist with fever and his mouth hanging open, Segelstein was astounded. "It was like lightning striking," he says. Next came "It's Hard to Be a Saint in the City," then "The E Street Shuffle." To Segelstein Bruce seemed electrified, so alive in his music that he was lighting up the entire auditorium. "I was gobsmacked and I'm not even a fan," Segelstein says now. He'd seen a lot of shows already, not just run-of-the-mill ones, either. Segelstein's dad worked in the industry and had access to nearly every important pop culture event his kids might find interesting. This had been going on since the early winter of 1964, when James was in grade school and his dad had arranged for him to sit in the audience of *The Ed Sullivan Show* the night the Beatles made their American debut. Then came shows with the Rolling Stones, Bob Dylan, Simon & Garfunkel, and on. So James Segelstein would not be easily impressed by anyone, particularly in the middle of a long, achy night when he would have been so much better off at home in bed. So what was he doing up on his feet, shouting and pumping his fist in the air? He still shakes his head when he recalls that night. "I can't think of any other show that left me quite the same way."

Mike Appel says now it was all part of his plan. That Bruce should sit down with the kid from the Brown University newspaper and really let it all hang out. Lay out everything about how Columbia Records was treating him, how the shift in management, the firing of Clive Davis and installation of Irwin Segelstein into the chief executive's chair, had resulted in Bruce being demoted from being the company's golden boy, *the next Bob Dylan!,* to being its least loved problem child. How the new executives had such little interest in Bruce and his work that they were avoiding his manager's calls and then, when they finally did pick up, refusing to cut the check Bruce needed to fund the recording of his next album. That they were, for all intents and purposes, torpedoing his career.

And that's exactly what Bruce did after the music died down and the ecstatic students floated out of Alumnae Hall. He toweled off, changed his shirt, grabbed a Coke, and hunkered down with John Garrett Andrews and Tom Miller, a freelancer on assignment from *Oui*. Bruce waited until Miller turned on his tape recorder and then fielded all the young reporters' questions about his work and current status, along with his opinion of the Columbia Records executives' attitudes. And he spoke clearly. So very clearly.

"We don't see eye to eye on a lot of things," Bruce said of the men now running his record label. "What it is is that Columbia picks a few people every once in a while and they're nice to a few people and shit on everyone else."

A hit artist like Tammy Wynette, Andrews offered, can probably get away with anything.

Bruce nodded and sighed. "Well yeah, if you sell records, you get a standing ovation when you walk in the building, you know. But I don't sell a lot of records yet."

What's worse, he continued, was that now the executives expected to dictate what he recorded and how. That was catastrophic for an artist like Bruce, who needed the freedom to express himself honestly and artistically.

"They want to stick their fingers in my pie. I don't need it, you know. Let me alone. Just let me make my music and leave me alone. They're bugging me for a single, a forty-five. I don't know, maybe they mean well, man, but I doubt it. You know it's like . . ." Bruce laughed and shook his head. "Ahhh, I don't know. I don't want to go into it if someone's not here to defend themselves."

But it wasn't the first time Bruce had aired out his frustrations in front of reporters. He'd described the same conflict to *The Boston Globe*'s William Howard a week before he got to Brown, complaining about how his own record company wouldn't let him do his job. Which in this case meant making a new record. "At least not until we deliver a new single," Bruce told Howard. "And we were all set to go back into the studios next week. Imagine that! It's like a publisher demanding a middle chapter [from an author] before agreeing to accept a novel."

The *Globe* published the story a week before Bruce got to Brown, and it was surely seen by thousands or even tens of thousands of readers. James Segelstein, the son of the record guy, hadn't been one of them. But he saw Andrews's interview that ran in the Brown University *Daily Herald* after the show that made such a big impact on him. When he made his next weekly call home to catch up with his parents James made a point of telling his dad about the show he'd seen and the interview Bruce gave to the school paper later that night.

I just saw that guy perform and he gave the greatest concert, James told Irwin Segelstein, the recently appointed president of Columbia Records. *This was literally the best concert I've ever seen.*

Irwin, a longtime executive at CBS Television, was unaccustomed to his children having such strong feelings about what was going on in his office. He made a note and put the issue on his to-do list.

Several East Coast schools held spring carnivals on the same weekend, so the band left Brown University soon after their midnight show, heading first to Storrs, Connecticut, for an outdoor show at the University of Connecticut the next afternoon, then to the University of Hartford in Hartford, Connecticut, thirty miles away, to open for the Chambers Brothers and the rock band Mountain for an evening show in the school's athletic center. From there they packed up and headed straight to Swarthmore, Pennsylvania, 230 miles away, for an afternoon show at Swarthmore College. Night after night, show after show, convert after convert. This was the work, and Bruce loved to work.

Mike Appel was with them all weekend, and as the musicians were limbering up for their set at the Scott Outdoor Amphitheater Bruce went up to his manager and told him to keep his ears open. They were going to play "Born to Run" for the first time, and he wanted him to give it a close listen and tell him how it sounded. Also, he'd rewritten the lyrics again, and so pay attention to those, too, okay? Appel nodded, sure, of course. They opened with a blazing "Does This Bus Stop at 82nd Street?," then played an assortment of 1974-era standbys, "Kitty's Back," "Spirit in the Night," the extended, guitar-heavy arrangement of "Blinded by the Light," then a special Clemons lead vocal, "Gimme That Wine," before Bruce made a quick count-off and the band dove straight into the opening bars of "Born to Run."

Appel had heard Bruce sketch the song on his acoustic guitar and heard the band working on the arrangement in the studio, so he knew its basic construction. He could hear the drums and guitar, the way the riff detonated the thing, and how Carter's drumming felt like an avalanche coming down a mountain, only in perfect time.

As heard through the concert speakers outdoors on a windy afternoon, it was harder to grasp the words. Appel could make out the chorus, that big *Baby, we were born to run* . . . But the rest of the lyrics were hard to decipher. "It was outdoors and the wind was blowing across the microphone," he recalls. Even so, the audience gave the unfamiliar song a good ovation, so that was encouraging.

What Appel might not have made out was how the lyrics of the song, its animating spirit, were beginning to brighten. The darkness in the piece persisted, but maybe something else glimmered on the horizon. Maybe it was just hope.

Irwin Segelstein called Mike Appel and caught the manager at his desk. A few days had passed since the midnight concert at Alumnae Hall and Bruce's pointed interview in the *Brown Daily Herald*. The executive might have found a copy of the paper, or maybe he'd just heard enough from James to know that one of his artists was telling the world how unhappy he was at Columbia and needed to be talked down from what could blow up into a potentially embarrassing public conflict. It was precisely the sort of spectacle Segelstein had been installed to avoid, so he got Appel's number, picked up the phone, and dialed.

Appel knew who Segelstein was, but they'd never spoken before and so the manager was surprised to find himself talking directly to the record company's new president.

The way Appel recalls it, he played the executive like a finely tuned fiddle. How was Segelstein doing? *Not great,* he responded. *Did your client really tell a reporter at Brown University that I won't let him record his next album?*

Appel tells the story with a sly grin, recalling how he made sympathetic noises, said yeah, that was rough, and he hoped that would be the end of that, but gee, Bruce was about to do an interview with *Rolling Stone,* and who knew what he'd tell them, or what the magazine would do with it. You know rock 'n' roll kids these days, so anti-authority and anti-business. Who knew what they'd do if an artist as critically celebrated as Bruce Springsteen were seen as being abused by corporate greed-heads? Well, it might get sticky.

At which point Segelstein, in Appel's memory, invited him and his lawyer to meet him for lunch the next day. Mercurio's on Fiftieth. *And bring Bruce, too.*

Sure, of course, Appel said. He rang off and sat back with a big smile on his face. He had made up the part about the *Rolling Stone* interview—no such interview was on the books, or even under discussion. But you do what you gotta do.

When the appointed time came the next day, Appel, his lawyer, Jules Kurz, and Bruce walked in, right on time. Segelstein, a distinctly nonglamorous middle-aged fellow with a beard and thick glasses whose years in television had made him accustomed to showbiz folks operating on their own schedule, was delighted. "Right on time!" he said. Sitting in his living room now, Bruce nods and gives a little shrug. "Irwin from the TV department, right? He had enough sense to know he had no sense of music." Segelstein and Appel got through the pleasantries, then it was Bruce's turn to talk. He didn't hold back. "We just let them know that we'd been let down by the record company, and we'd been having a lot of trouble communicating to the guys who were now running the place," Bruce says. "And he said, 'Well, what can we do to fix this? How can we make it right?'"

Appel knew exactly what it would take. Bruce needed to make his next album; they needed their advance money to make it happen.

Segelstein nodded. "Well," he said, "why don't we get Bruce Springsteen back into the studio?"

Appel smiled. "Oh boy, you're not gonna get any problems from me!" he said. "That sounds like a great idea! You should run a record company!" Segelstein smiled and lit a cigarette.

"He was a square guy," Bruce says. "But also a square shooter."

Segelstein pledged to cut loose the money Bruce would need to fund recording sessions for his next record. Whether it would be enough to make the album he was envisioning was another matter. To say nothing of the money he, the band, their crew, and Appel needed to pay the rent, buy groceries, and cover all the other costs of living. And no matter what Segelstein had said, no matter his intentions, Charles Koppelman was still the head of Columbia's artists & repertoire department and was still charged with making the decisions about the artists they kept on the label, and what their records should look and sound like. And as far as he was concerned Bruce Springsteen was still on the list of also-ran artists the company could, and probably should, drop from its roster.

Chapter 6

Rock 'n' Roll Future

Bruce kept going back to "Born to Run." He got it to the point where the music felt right, the simple chords on the verse contrasting with the head-spinning changes in the bridge, the tension building with every upward step, then rocketing downward again, only to speed off into the final verse.

> *We gotta live with the sadness*
> *Drive to this madness*
> *Oh burnin' off the radio*
> *Oh well maybe someday girl I'll get us somewhere*
> *We'll get to that place we really wanna go*
> *And we'll walk in the sun*

The darkness was still there, along with the doubt and fear. "I was a romantic at heart, you know," Bruce says. "So a dark romantic, I guess." And yet he kept finding room for hope. You had to have hope, if only because your heart was beating and your feet were still on the ground. "I remember it coming slowly. And it took me a lot of pages to write." But it kept coming. And sometimes, if he gazed deep enough into the inky night, he could glimpse a little light.

Bruce was not the only young man pondering existential matters in the spring of 1974. And though there were plenty of reasons to feel unsure about the fate of the nation—the Nixonian cancer in the presidency, the staggered economy, the choked gasoline supply and the threat it posed to the basic American impulse to keep moving—some people didn't have to look beyond their own lives to feel doubtful. The pivot from youth to adulthood, from the first rush of independence to the more complicated satisfactions of full-grown maturity, could be tricky. Particularly for young men whose ambitions seemed an impossible distance from their grasp.

Was the pursuit of rock 'n' roll glory a worthwhile quest for a mature, even intelligent, person to make the center of his life? And what if you didn't make music but spent your time listening to and writing about it? Jon Landau had spent the better part of ten years with pop music at the center of his life, playing guitar and performing with a band called the Jelly Roll during his college years at Brandeis, then as a critic, contributing album reviews to *Crawdaddy*, the fledgling rock journal started by Paul Williams, then in a more ambitious rock 'n' roll / youth culture magazine starting up in San Francisco: *Rolling Stone*.

Landau was a gifted writer and a thoughtful critic, but his heart was never entirely in letters. He wanted to get his hands on music, wanted to help shape sound and guide musicians toward the fullest expression of their artistry. He produced an album for the revolutionary Detroit rockers the MC5, then one for singer-songwriter Livingston Taylor (younger brother of James). An album he was working on with the J. Geils Band fell apart, and then when Landau was diagnosed with Crohn's disease, a painful intestinal ailment, he went back to writing.

Landau was a prominent critic with real influence with readers and in the entertainment industry. He was, arguably, one of the two or three most powerful music writers in the nation, a thought that tickled him so much he started referring to himself as the King, rivaling Robert Christgau's claim of being Dean of the American Rock Critics. Those serious rock critics in the early '70s were not shy about asserting their primacy. But by 1974 popular music was leaving Landau cold. The explosive creativity and sense of sociopolitical mission that animated pop during the 1960s had ebbed. Meanwhile the cynicism leaching into the culture in the wake of the hippie era's unfulfilled idealism sapped his spirit. "There are months when I hate it, going through the routine just as a shoe salesman goes through his," he wrote at the time. "But in my own moments of greatest need, I never give up the search for sounds that can answer every impulse, consume all emotion, cleanse and purify—all things that we have no right to expect from even the greatest works of art but which we can occasionally derive from them."

All of this, along with some growing doubts about his own life and reason for existing, was in his mind when Landau slouched into the Harvard Square Theatre on May 9, almost exactly a month since the critic had seen Bruce for the first time. It was after 9 p.m.—he'd opted to see Bruce perform the second of the two shows he was playing that night. Landau came in hoping for something more meaningful than two hours of ordinary rock 'n' roll. His Crohn's disease had diminished his energy and sapped the color from his days. His marriage to the film critic Janet Maslin was faltering. And if that weren't bad enough, it was the eve of his twenty-seventh birthday. Just as Landau needed to summon the energy to confront what felt like encroaching middle age, he could sense his passion for life fading away.

The lights went down and the show began. And for Landau, and eventually the man who was just stepping onto the stage, nothing would ever be quite the same.

Bruce knew Landau would be in the audience. Maybe that's why the set list began with the slowed-down arrangement of "E Street

Shuffle," a leisurely version of his musical statement of purpose, the loving description of Saturday night in an Asbury Park bar, where the day-to-day loses its grip and music makes the world incandesce. Next came "New York City Serenade," Sancious's dramatic Mozart-meets-Monk piano opening giving way to Bruce's tale of the city's predawn life, concluding with a tender portrait of his odd but loving grandfather, who found his living in the cast-off belongings of others. *Listen to your junk man,* Bruce whispered, *he's singing, singing, singing.* Then came the rockers: "Spirit in the Night" and "It's Hard to Be a Saint in the City," both performed with feral intensity. Next came a reeling performance of "Kitty's Back," before he turned down the fire for the bittersweet tale of boardwalk life "4th of July, Asbury Park (Sandy)." And every few songs a peek into Bruce's next album. Definitely "Born to Run," possibly the debut of the mini-epic "Jungleland," maybe the one he called "Angel Baby," possibly one of the early versions of the made-for-the-bars rave-up "A Love So Fine" (a.k.a. "A Night Like This"). Then the blow-out-the-jams set closers, "Rosalita," a solo piano performance of "For You," then a full-band, everyone-up-and-dancing, show-stopping sprint through the Isley Brothers–by–way–of–the–Beatles' "Twist and Shout." Everyone was on their feet by then, and nobody was dancing as hard, or screaming as loud, as Jon Landau.

Hours later Landau was at his desk at home, wide awake, trying to translate everything he was feeling into words. It was like he'd sent a distress signal out into the ether, desperately seeking life-changing rock 'n' roll, and unexpectedly, magically, had it answered in the most overwhelming way imaginable.

He wrote, in a review that would be published in the Boston alternative newspaper *The Real Paper,* "When his two-hour set ended I could only think, can anyone really be this good; can anyone say this much to me, can rock 'n' roll still speak with this kind of power and glory?"

His response had been visceral: "I felt the sores on my thighs where I had been pounding my hands in time for the entire concert and knew that the answer was yes . . . And on a night when I needed to feel young, he made me feel like I was hearing music for the very first time."

Landau didn't have a plan. But he knew exactly what he was doing. "It's something I've never quite come to terms with," he wrote to me in a 2012 email. "What I wanted you to know is, yes, I knew Bruce was in trouble at Columbia. I knew I had a pretty big voice over there. I was a leading critic, and I knew everyone [at Columbia] was going to read what I said, from top to bottom."

Watching Bruce onstage, hearing his songs, sensing everything he felt for rock 'n' roll, how much of himself he put into his performance and his evocation of the form's power—artistic, personal, social, political—was like having a dream he'd been carrying for more than a decade come to life. He said it himself: *power and glory*. Words meant to describe a ruler or a holy figure.

I wasn't expecting the email from Landau. I turned on my computer one morning and it was waiting for me, almost as if Landau had written it at 4 a.m. too, the way he'd written that fateful review in 1974, gazing out of a rain-streaked window with music playing in his ears. He'd just read his most famous column again, he told me, for the first time in years. He had come to feel a little sheepish about what he'd put into print that morning . . . decades of experience, everything that had happened to him since that long-ago birthday morning, had made him cringe over how much of himself he had revealed. The emotional neediness, the awed tone, the vivid evocation of the author's angst and deliverance via rock 'n' roll shamanism. I mean, *yeeeesh*, right? Except to hell with being embarrassed over having a feeling. "I thought, well, this is me at twenty-seven, doing a whole lot of things at once. Writing my heart out, a really naked piece of writing. And doing it in a very self-obsessed way, with the energy of a teenager. And the main thing I realized, and I've spoken about this a time or two . . . is that I wouldn't change a word of it."

Not a word. Especially not the ones that loomed above everything else. He didn't know it at the time; there was no way he could have known it because the album didn't exist. But what he was feeling on that rainy spring morning was precisely what Bruce was yearning to express on his next record. And on every record he'd make after that.

"I saw rock and roll future and its name is Bruce Springsteen."

Just that. Just the thing that mattered to him the most.

And just as Landau had intended, these words would change the course of his life, of Bruce's life and career, the course of rock 'n' roll, popular culture, and, when you consider the artist's impact on society and politics, the culture of the United States of America.

That may be a little over-the-top. But going over the top is exactly what rock 'n' roll, Bruce Springsteen, and *Born to Run,* in particular, are all about.

Photograph © by Barry Schneier

Chapter 7

Growing Young with Rock and Roll

After he'd finished the review, Landau went to bed, slept fitfully for a few hours, then went back to his typewriter to read over what he'd done. It looked different in the light of day. Some journalists could center their own experience in their stories; that was a central premise in the New Journalism being practiced at alternative publications like *Rolling Stone* and *The Real Paper,* where Landau's column appeared. Critics certainly wrote from their individual experience of the art they were addressing. But the usual critical voice had an overarching tone of erudition and expertise. The supreme confidence of the omniscient. And this was exactly the opposite of that: vulnerable, wounded, desperate for salvation. Looking for clearer eyes, Landau turned to Dave Marsh, the fellow music critic who had more or less dragged him to his first Springsteen show a month earlier. Marsh also knew a thing or two about balancing the personal voice with the critical pose of omniscient expertise, so Landau handed him his manuscript and asked him to take a look. *I'm not sure if we should run this,* he said.

He left Marsh alone to read, and when his fellow critic tracked him down fifteen minutes later he handed the papers back with an answer. "I was twenty-four at the time and also feeling old," Marsh told me in 2010. "So I said, 'I just read it and I *know* we should print it.'"

Headlined "Growing Young with Rock and Roll," Landau's column ran in the May 22 issue of *The Real Paper*. Although it appeared in an alternative weekly seen almost exclusively by residents of Boston, you could get a subscription copy mailed nearly anywhere. Given the significance of Boston as a population center, and one rich in college students, more than a few of those were addressed to executives at Columbia Records in New York.

And just as he had suspected, Landau's words made an impact on the men who ran that company.

Some of them were already on the case. Al Teller, Frank Shargo, Ron Oberman, Michael Pillot, Peter Philbin, and Ron McCarrell, among others, were tracking the reviews that came in, particularly from live performances. They were among the younger staffers in the building, not decision-makers, per se, but when good notices about Bruce came in they made certain they were copied and distributed to the company's top executives. When word went out that spring that Bruce was on the verge of getting dropped by the label, Ron Oberman—the young publicist who was buttonholed by Hammond on his first day in the office during the summer of 1972, then was wowed by Bruce's nightclub set—composed a fiery page-and-a-half memo urging Koppelman to reconsider, got a dozen of his colleagues to cosign it, and sent it to all the top executives.

When Bruce's advocates saw Landau's *Real Paper* column about the future of rock 'n' roll, they shifted their lobbying campaign into higher gear. "Frank Shargo came in with the review and I read it and called in the product management team," recalls Al Teller. "I said, 'This is fucking great, this will kill all the bullshit. So let's just run with this.' And we did."

They worked up a set of advertisements for *The Wild, the Innocent and the E Street Shuffle* and had the company buy a full page in *Rolling Stone*—an extraordinary move for a failed album that was eight months old—with an engagingly moody photo of Bruce, the last six paragraphs of Landau's column, and, in a banner headline, the big cash-money quote: "I SAW ROCK 'N' ROLL FUTURE AND ITS NAME IS BRUCE SPRINGSTEEN." They put the same headline on a poster they printed and shipped to record stores and other sales points, with a big illustration of Bruce, another quote from Landau's column, and similarly over-the-top blurbs from critics published in *Crawdaddy*, *Stereo Review*, and *The National Observer*.

It was a far more significant advertising push than *The Wild, the Innocent* received when it had been released the previous November. But if the burst of publicity seemed to represent a complete turnaround in the senior executives' enthusiasm for Bruce Springsteen, it didn't. "It just didn't move the needle," says publicist Michael Pillot, the regional promotion man then working out of Texas. It didn't restore the buzz Bruce had at the company during Clive Davis's tenure in the president's office. And, most importantly, it didn't get Bruce's name off of Koppelman's drop list.

When the British writer Jerry Gilbert sat down with Bruce early in the summer of 1974, working on a feature for *ZigZag*, the musician was forthright about where his career stood. "We're at the lowest we've ever been right now," he said. They weren't making any money from their records, and Columbia wasn't providing any of the financial or promotional tour support bigger acts received. With no record royalties flowing in, and no one helping pay for publicity, hotels, or transportation on the road, the entire enterprise was forced to live hand-to-mouth. "If we don't play every week of the year then we don't have money," Bruce told Gilbert. "Right now we've just come off the road and the guys are getting thrown out of their houses."

But Bruce still had some aces tucked into his sleeve. David Bowie was interested in recording one or two of his songs, so that could bring in some money. And of course, Bruce was eager to get to work on his next album, too. "I'm still fooling with the words for the new single but I think it'll be good," he told Gilbert. "I've written a lot of stuff for the new album. I've got quite a few . . . when I get into the studio I'll have a clear picture."

They spent most of June and the first half of July at home, due in part to canceled shows in the South and to studio dates at the 914 recording studio, the relatively inexpensive facility in Blauvelt, New York, about forty-five minutes outside of New York City, they had made the center of their recording operations. There Bruce and Mike worked to put the finishing touches on "Born to Run," the single that would, or wouldn't, convince the Columbia executives not just to fork over the money to make his third album, but to actually support the project throughout the recording, release, and promotional stages, in ways that actually fit the artist he was, the music he was making, and the audience it needed to reach. All of that was still unresolved, as was the source of the money they needed to keep their entire organization—musicians, crew, management—afloat while they devoted all their time to the recording sessions.

Whatever money they got from the label to make the single, which wasn't close to enough to pay for the band's living and tour expenses, had long since run dry, and with the recording advance set aside for the production of the new album, Appel dug into his own accounts to pay the bills. When they burned through that money, Louis Lahav, 914's staff engineer and their collaborator on virtually every note Bruce had recorded, stepped in to help, neglecting to submit work orders for his efforts and equipment use, and sneaking the musicians into the facility after midnight, when the place was supposed to be closed and studio owner Brooks Arthur would never know what they were up to. This nearly led to disaster one night when Arthur showed up unexpectedly and found them all there. He was understandably irate, but Lahav talked Arthur down and promised never to do it again.

Whether Lahav kept that promise or not is debatable. What was increasingly clear to the engineer is that his allegiance had shifted—from Arthur, 914, and his own career to Bruce Springsteen and his music. "It was like a religion, almost," says Lahav, who had moved to the United States from Israel to pursue a career in recording. "We all believed it, you know. And it was like, very, very fast becoming like a cult." Bruce had a way of drawing people in and, in his way, ensorcelling them. To Lahav, it had less to do with the things Bruce said than the amount of time he spent saying nothing. "I remember Bruce had a lot of silent moments, where everybody was waiting for him while he was thinking or writing or working something out. Those intense moments that Bruce was into something. It became very clear how great an artist he is."

The sense of spiritual attachment was particularly intense for Stephen Appel, Mike's younger brother who joined the touring party after graduating high school in 1973. He began to feel Bruce's pull soon after he started spending time with the musician. "He had an unusual grip on me," he says. What hit him, Stephen continues, was how seriously the musician took himself. How his dedication to his craft completely overwhelmed any interest in the women, drugs, and partying other rock stars spent so much of their time chasing. "He felt a responsibility and it was a very serious one. And because he was that way, you kind of became that way, too. You were really being very serious about the work."

Bruce had long displayed a visceral grasp on performing, but by the summer of 1974, after a year and a half of nearly nonstop work on the road, he'd developed a more thoughtful approach. He constructed shows that were tighter, with a narrative focus he could adjust to fit the mood of the evening. Most nights he'd pull together a two-hour set that traveled through the stations of human experience (innocence, hope, love, loss, and joy) before lifting off into something like rock 'n' roll ecstasy. Word of the little-known rocker who could make an ordinary evening in a dingy nightclub feel like an encounter with the majestic rippled from each show he played. Vast regions of the country remained untouched, but the sections Bruce and his band had worked began to sprout followers. And though they hadn't focused much energy on New York City, word from the performances in the fringes of the metro area, and in nearby cities like Philadelphia and Boston, put Bruce in position to book three straight nights at the Bottom Line, a new but high-profile club near New York University in Greenwich Village, starting on July 12, 1974.

As in most cities where he wasn't established, the first shows in the four-hundred-seat venue—two an evening—didn't fill the house. Glen Brunman, the editor of a Long Island alternative weekly called *Good Times*, had heard some of Bruce's songs on the radio and liked them well enough, but Landau's *Real Paper* column, and the advertisements trumpeting his raves, catalyzed him into getting a ticket for the late performance on the twelfth.

It was crowded, the energy in the room closer to curious than wildly enthusiastic. Could this guy really be as great as the hype said he was? Judging from the conversations near the bar, a significant percentage of the night's patrons came looking to be won over. And then it was showtime.

The lights went down at 11:30 p.m., and after a brief opening set by the singer-songwriter Jeffrey Comanor, Bruce and the band stepped onto the stage. Sancious swept his hands around the piano keys, and Clemons hit a few notes on the saxophone while Bruce plugged in his guitar and turned it up. An offstage voice announced, *Ladies and gentlemen, Bruce Springsteen*, prompting applause and scattered cheers. Bruce opened with a song Brunman can't remember, but he never forgot what happened next. Bruce switched to a twelve-string guitar and launched into a simple four-note guitar riff, jangling, that Brunman thought he recognized. It was an oldie, a cover of the Crystals' "Then He Kissed Me," adjusted for Bruce's gender and orientation ("Then *she* kissed me"). As produced by Phil Spector, the original had the quasi-symphonic texture the producer favored:

layered percussion, the low end dense with basses and baritone saxophone, the high end stacked with guitars, strings, and background harmonies. Written for a teenage audience in 1963, the song might have seemed shockingly naïve to adult ears listening a dozen years later. It's about what sounds like a high school sock hop: A guy walks up to a girl, asks if she'd like to dance. They go to the floor, where feelings take wing. And by the time they walk home at the end of the evening it's true love. *All the stars were shining bright / And then she kissed me.*

In the wake of the 1960s, Woodstock, Vietnam, and a decade of rock 'n' roll songs that served as broadsides in a countercultural revolution, the Crystals' "Then He Kissed Me," along with all the early rock 'n' roll that had been made for teenyboppers of the '50s and early '60s, would be relegated to oldies fests or to tongue-in-cheek revivalists like Sha Na Na. You'd never expect to hear that kind of song coming from an up-and-coming artist—certainly not one who had been celebrated as the new Bob Dylan. But just as Brunman recognized the song as a dusty old girl-group hit, Bruce, whose twelve-string electric gave the opening riff the sound of pure, delicious jangle pop, underscored by Clemons's baritone sax and Carter's timpani-like pounds on his floor tom and then amplified by Bruce's gritty, impassioned vocal, gave the old song a wall-rattling kind of gravitas. Because he performed it with as much passion and dedication as any song he ever sang.

The rest of the show was just as impressive, and by the time he got home Brunman had an entirely new appreciation for Bruce, and for rock 'n' roll. Once again, word of the show spread and both of the Saturday performances were sold out. Bruce opened the late show with "Then She Kissed Me," then swung into a tight program that took a turn about thirty-five minutes in when he introduced a new song: "This is something called 'Jungleland.'" There was no applause, just silent anticipation. Sancious played a brief, unformed piano introduction, resolving into a chiming figure that repeated as Bruce stood at the microphone, eyes closed, setting the scene for the Magic Rat and the barefoot girl as they come together, climb into his car, and drive away to meet their fate in the big city. Their adventure built the song to full blast, then faded to a whisper before ending with Sancious alone at the piano, a sweet bluesy riff tumbling down to a resolution that the crowd, which had grown quietly electrified, greeted with an ovation. When that ended Bruce set up another new one: "This is our new single, hot off the racks," he said, half-joking. "So you can listen for it any day now." He picked out a few notes on his guitar. "It's called 'Tramps Like Us, Born to Run.'" Which wasn't the title, but Carter blasted the drum intro, the band ripped into the opening, and Bruce sailed into the verse. When it ended the ovation rivaled the volume of the song, the throng not just applauding but whistling, stomping, and cheering as if he'd just played an old favorite that they'd been yearning to hear for years.

Chapter 8

Walk with Me Out on the Wire

Eventually the labor on the "Born to Run" single came down to recording overdubs and the vocal. Ensconced in 914 in the wee hours, Appel and Bruce seemed to try every idea that occurred to them. A string section. An ascending guitar riff repeating through the verse. A chorus of women chiming in on the chorus. An even bigger chorus of women oooh-ing behind the third verse. Still more strings on the bridge and on the last verse, doing those disco-style swoops, like sciroccos whipping up from the dance floor. They'd work out a part, hire whatever musicians or singers were needed to get it on tape, then mix it all together to see what they had. Sometimes it would stick, sometimes they'd just laugh, shake their heads, and slice it out. How about a second vocal on the verses? Bruce tried that, harmonizing with himself. They mixed it in, listened to what they had, and . . . um, nope. Bruce knew exactly what he wanted for the saxophone break, so that part was easy. Then he spent ages working on it with Clemons, eight, ten, maybe twelve hours, playing the same notes over and over again, Bruce looking for a slightly different feel, a slightly different tone, a tiny adjustment to the rhythm of this passage, this pair of notes, this portion of that note. When that was done they turned their attention once again to the backing track. Adding more keyboards, taking them out, then putting some of them back in and trying again. Hmmmm, maybe turn up the guitars a tick?

Work on the instrumental track went on and on, but it still didn't rival Bruce's laboring over the lyrics. He had always put energy into his narratives but the pressure he felt to get "Born to Run" just exactly right pushed him to a whole other level of perfectionism, determined to get every word, every nuance, every syllable, something like flawless. No, *exactly* flawless. Sometimes he'd be in the midst of a take, sing a few lines of a verse, shake it off, then take his notebook to a folding chair. He'd find a pen, open the book, look at the page, and just . . . think. He'd be there for a while. An hour, two hours, maybe more. Meanwhile in the control room Appel would be at his place at the board, Louis Lahav in his. This happened a lot. How long would it be this time? They'd peer through the glass, chat a bit. Fiddle with paperwork, try to see what Bruce was up to. Still staring into space? Reading back through his pages? Writing? Impatience was not an option. Appel was paying the bills but as far as he was concerned Bruce could have all the time he needed. Eventually he'd look up, reach for his headphones, and say he was ready to record. Lahav would roll the tape and they'd begin again.

What made it worthwhile was that the lyrics were improving so dramatically. A song that had started as a nearly surrealist portrait of a world gone mad—the racers run down by their own cars, the highway buckling beneath their mag wheels, the thrill-kill junkies gunning down soldiers *just for the noise / Not even for the kicks*— had been remade into a vibrant highway saga that, while heavily symbolic, could be recognized as existing on the modern Jersey Shore. The cars roaring down Highway 9, the arcade games in the Palace on the Asbury Park boardwalk, the roller coaster standing sentry over the couples on a fog-shrouded nighttime beach. The physical world hung together, but only just. The cars were suicide machines. The homes they lived in were cages, the towns spiritual death traps. Meanwhile, the nation spun crazily toward some kind of doom. *We've gotta get out while we're young,* Bruce sang, and the urgency in his voice was echoed by every note and drum stroke, the hard edge in the guitar, the cry of the organ, the growl and wail of the saxophone. But now the horror that fueled the original drafts had been eclipsed by something more powerful: the singer's love for the woman he now referred to as Wendy.

And who is she? Bruce's lyric reveals next to nothing: not what she looks like, not where she's from, nothing about the currents that have pulled her into the night and into his arms. None of it could matter more than the simple fact of their connection. In a rush, he confesses everything: he's scared and lonely, he's never been in love and has no idea what it's like. But he's determined to escape their fallen city and he's convinced his only way out is to take her with him. *I'll love you with all the madness in my soul,* he swears. He is so ready to move that by the second verse the narrator and car seem to have merged: *Just wrap your legs 'round these velvet rims / And strap your hands across my engines.* He opens the door, urges her aboard, every sinew straining to deliver them both to . . . where, exactly? *That place where we really want to go,* he says, not exactly narrowing it down. How could it matter? The beauty they're chasing has nothing to do with where they land and everything to do with having the courage to make the leap.

Finally the song felt finished. Now it was August 1974, right around the time of President Nixon's resignation. The denouement of the Watergate scandal—what the freshly anointed, sweeter-spirited President Gerald Ford called *our long national nightmare*—lifted at least a part of the nation's psychic burden. Suddenly the breeze carried a sense of new beginnings, of progress, of the universe tilting, in its nearly imperceptible way, toward justice. A propitious time to move forward. They made a final mix and dubbed it onto a cassette. Appel put the thing into his pocket and he and Bruce walked from the manager's midtown office up to the CBS building on West Fifty-Seventh Street. Bruce decided to wait in the lobby downstairs while Appel carried the tape up to the executive floor. Appel found his way to the office of Steve Popovich, a friendly artists & repertoire executive he hoped would help overwhelm the doubts of A & R chief Charles Koppelman.

Popovich was busy when Appel came knocking, but he beckoned the manager into his office, took the cassette from his hand, and spun his chair to face the tape deck on the shelf. A big moment! Except Appel couldn't help but notice that the executive's telephone was off the hook, sitting on his desk as if he were in the middle of a conversation. And not just one phone, either. The way Appel tells the story, Popovich was working three phones at the same time: one on his right ear, another on his left, a third handset on the desk in front of him. He told one, or maybe all of them, to hang on for a second, slapped the tape in, and hit play. A moment of silence, then the drums, the guitar, the full band playing full blast over the speakers. Appel sat back, peering into the executive's face, hoping to see a glimmer of . . . something. Popovich listened for a few moments, then went back to the conversations he was having with whoever was hanging on the other end of his telephones. Picked up the one that was resting on his desk and said something to that person, then picked up the second, then the third. And when "Born to Run" finished playing four minutes later he was still talking. Eventually Appel caught his eye and Popovich let the mouthpieces droop from his mouth. So . . . what'd he think, Appel asked, and the executive kind of shrugged. "He said, 'I liked the riff. It's all right, but I didn't digest the rest,'" Appel recalls. "I said, 'Why don't I digest some more myself? Like, we just finished it ourselves. And then we'll come back to you with some other suggestions.' He said, 'Anytime, Mike!' And then he got right back to talking into his phones."

Popovich was a smart and soulful guy; he and Appel had been friends for years. Appel and Bruce had walked into the building hoping that "Born to Run" would catalyze him, that he'd be so crazy about the song he would play it for Koppelman and all the other top executives and get *them* so excited about it that they'd not only marshal all their enthusiasm for Bruce's next album but also rush-release the song as a stand-alone single they would push onto all the big stations. A shot across the bow of the entire music industry, letting them know exactly why the august critic Jon Landau had written that Bruce was the future of rock 'n' roll. Then they'd finish the album, Columbia would catapult it into the marketplace with enough velocity for it to carom into the hands of a million new fans. That's what they had hoped, anyway.

Appel rode the elevator back to the lobby, where he found Bruce reclining on a sofa. The musician hopped to his feet when he saw his manager, and when they were close enough to speak he had only one question: "So?" Appel shrugged and gave it to him straight. That Popovich had only sort of listened, then said he hadn't been able to absorb it. Appel: "Bruce said, 'So now what are we going to do?' So I said, 'Let me go back to my office, you go back to Asbury Park. And if you get any brainstorm or if I do, we'll call each other.'" They walked the next few blocks together before parting at Fifty-Fifth Street, Appel heading to his office and Bruce continuing downtown to the Port Authority and his bus back to the Jersey Shore. He wouldn't have gotten very far before a new plan of attack revealed itself to Appel. It would require them to take a leap, and to risk aggravating the living shit out of the very executives who could help, or hinder, them the most. A career-sized risk, in other words. What else was new. The only question in Appel's mind was how quickly he could get it done.

There's such a fine line between evangelism and insanity. Between giving your heart and losing your mind. What drew Bruce to Appel, back when he first played him the crop of songs he'd written in the beginning of 1972, was that the man clearly had no conception of where that boundary might fall. "His heart was in it, and everything else," Bruce told me in 2011. "That's part of what attracted me, because it was all or nothing."

Born in Queens in 1942, Mike was the eldest of the five children of Thomas and Marie Appel. Thomas was all business, building a real estate company successful enough to propel his young family into the comfortable Long Island village of Old Brookville. He expected a lot from his kids, and even more from his oldest son, from whom he didn't spare the rod. "Dad had a tough relationship with all of us, but Mike really bore the brunt of the physicality," his younger brother Stephen recalls. "The hitting." Marie did her best to assuage her son's feelings. Once a singer and performer herself, she recognized Mike's musicality and encouraged it, first buying him an acoustic guitar and, when he became a rock 'n' roll obsessive, an electric Silvertone with an amplifier.

He started his first band when he was in high school and was its uncontested leader, running the rehearsals, writing the songs, nailing down engagements, and cultivating the connections required to record demos, finally earning a contract with one of 20th Century Fox's smaller rock labels. The Humbugs were an instrumental band, and their songs were catchy enough for one or two to gain a footing on the regional sales charts. After high school Appel majored in business at St. John's University and when he realized that graduation would make him a target for the military draft, he figured out he could sidestep the battlefield in Vietnam by joining a reserve unit of the US Marines and leveraging his college diploma into an office job. His plan worked perfectly. After a few months of basic training on Parris Island, Appel was back on Long Island, with only a few years of monthly service weekends standing between him and the end of his brush with the United States military.

Splayed between the blossoming youth culture of 1967 and the hard-ass principles he'd learned from his father and the drill sergeants of the US Marines, Appel formed a hippie-ish band called the Balloon Farm and wrote a psychedelic garage rock tune called "A Question of Temperature" that rose into the Top 40 in 1968 and led to a songwriting deal with a production company. There he met another young songwriter named Jimmy Cretecos, and they formed a partnership they took to Wes Farrell's music production house, where he got them working on his central pursuit, providing hit songs for the stars of ABC's rock music sitcom *The Partridge Family*. They wrote one significant hit for the group, "Doesn't Somebody Want to Be Wanted," which rose to number 6 on the *Billboard* Hot 100 in 1971, along with an array of others, but Appel and Cretecos had ambitions that went far beyond writing pop hits. They also wanted to produce records and to become managers, perhaps with a stable of acts whose songs they would write or produce or both. They were only just launching this part of their business when Bruce Springsteen carried his guitar into their office. They both heard greatness in his songs. Neither hesitated to quit his job with Farrell and put all their chips on the young New Jersey musician. But Appel took the lead in virtually everything he did, and his dedication to Bruce was no different.

From the moment they began, there was nothing Appel wouldn't do for Bruce, no outrageous thing he wouldn't say, no wild stunt he wouldn't try to pull to get Bruce the breaks and attention he knew his client deserved. Cold-calling John Hammond to land an audition was crazy enough; when they got in the door Appel snarled at the storied music executive, essentially ordering the man who had discovered Benny Goodman, Billie Holiday, Bob Dylan, and a legion of other culture-defining musicians to sign Bruce on the spot, lest he be revealed as a has-been. Hammond tolerated the abuse, but only just. Once *Greetings* was released and Bruce started performing, Appel's approach to music writers and editors was less a pitch than a full-throated harangue. He did the same to Columbia Records executives he deemed insufficiently focused on his client. When he came on the road with his client, Appel dealt with club owners and promoters by donning a US Marines drill sergeant's hat and screaming at any and everyone who displeased him. Toting up the numbers of radio programmers who had given Bruce a chance in 1973 (not many), Appel bought sacks of charcoal briquets, had them individually wrapped, and mailed them to the worst offenders at Christmas, with cards explaining why

Santa was putting coal in their stockings. It was pretty funny if you looked at it right; most of the recipients didn't see it that way.

Not long after that, Appel came up with his Super Bowl idea. Granted, the NFL championship game of the early 1970s wasn't quite the national-holiday-sized event it is now, but it was still a pretty big deal, and so try to imagine the thought process that led to Appel ringing up a producer at CBS, the guy in charge of planning the network's coverage of the big game, to pitch the idea of having his client Bruce Springsteen launch the proceedings by standing with his guitar on the fifty-yard line and performing his new antiwar song, "Balboa vs. the Earth Slayer." This at a time when professional football existed cultural light-years from pop music, and several decades before even the most overwhelmingly popular artists would be invited to perform during the halftime break. To imagine the biggest, most conservative television network of all would cede five minutes of broadcast time, let alone Super Bowl time, to a skinny, bearded, decidedly unpopular folk singer from New Jersey and his metaphorical song about the wickedness of President Nixon's Vietnam policies . . . well, no. Never. Not in a million goddamn years. That is lunatic thinking. Reflect on this to Appel now and he just shrugs. "Was I too aggressive or outlandish in how I managed Bruce? People say that, especially when it comes to the Super Bowl thing," he says. "But that crazy, reaching-for-the-stars attitude permeated everything in the early years."

So the Columbia execs couldn't be bothered to listen to Bruce's new song? They didn't care enough about his career to get "Born to Run" out into the world and show the world exactly what rock 'n' roll's future was going to sound like? Well, fuck that. As far as Mike was concerned, Bruce Springsteen shouldn't have to take *no* from anybody. Neither would Mike Appel.

Chapter 9

Welcome to E Street

And still, the setbacks kept coming.

The New York shows at the Bottom Line nightclub in mid-July felt like a turning point. They'd ended up packing the place. The reaction, and the reviews, were triumphant. And the energy had stayed just as high when they rolled out the new songs. "Born to Run" went off like a stick of dynamite, and "Jungleland," with all its musical twists and turns and a narrative that spiraled through the city following its hero from fragile hope to utter desolation, triggered one of those ovations that takes a moment to start, then goes on and on. The band was in top form, and the Columbia executives who dotted the room, and not just the usual young apostles, had seemed impressed by what they'd seen. It had been a pivotal night for David Sancious too, and this created still another hurdle for Bruce to clear.

Sancious was backstage after the set one night when he was approached by an A & R executive from Epic Records, another music industry subsidiary in the CBS empire. When Bruce was working on his first solo songs, when nearly all of his bandmates had relocated to Richmond, Virginia, Sancious had put together a trio with Boom Carter and Garry Tallent to play his original jazz fusion songs. They'd recorded a demo, which had found its way to Epic, and into this guy's office. And now he was wondering if the pianist was interested in making another demo and, perhaps, signing with Epic. Sancious was very interested in doing that, and when the guy liked what he heard and offered him a recording contract, he took it. Which meant he had to leave Bruce's band. That would have been a hard enough blow for Bruce to absorb but what made it even tougher was that Sancious would be taking his drummer, Ernest "Boom" Carter, whom he'd played music with since they were kids, with him.

Bruce couldn't begrudge his bandmates' shot with their own band. Both were talented musicians and Sancious, in particular, was so extravagantly gifted it was hard to imagine he'd settle for being a sideman in someone else's rock 'n' roll band for very long. Bruce made certain to give him plenty of room to shine during the band's shows—his largely improvised introduction to "New York City Serenade" grew into a showcase segment, including sections he performed in part leaning inside his instrument, plucking the piano strings with his fingers. Sancious was perfectly capable of playing straight rock too, but that obviously wasn't where his heart resided, and when he came to Bruce with news of his offer from Epic, Bruce leaped up and gave him a hug, along with his blessings.

"Oh man, I wanted to cry because he was so good," Bruce says. "And we were such good friends. We bunked together for the whole year he was in the band, and I loved him. And then he took Boom with him, and Boom had assimilated himself into the band in a lovely way." The dual departures also disrupted the band's racial balance. "We were three Black guys and three white guys playing a mixture of rock and soul music. It was a lovely little band, and so I hated to see it disintegrate."

One of Sancious and Carter's final shows with the band was the highest-profile show they'd ever played, a set at the Schaefer Music Festival, held at Wollman Rink in New York's Central Park on August 3. Bruce was the secondary performer on the bill, beneath headliner Anne Murray, the Canadian singer who was coming off her most recent top ten single, a smooth cover of the Beatles' "You Won't See Me." Murray had sold more records than Bruce, but the intensity of his performances, and the fervent pitch of his following in the Northeast, had inspired Appel to approach her manager and urge him to switch her headlining set to the middle of the show, and let Bruce close the evening with his raucous, crowd-riling rock 'n' roll. Murray's people gave it some thought, then opted to err on the side of the pop charts and said naw, she'll be fine. This proved a crucial error, as Bruce's set, and particularly the closing showstoppers "Kitty's Back" and "Rosalita," drew the New York crowd to their feet, dancing wildly and screaming for more. Murray came smiling and twinkling out a few minutes later, but the heavily Bruce-centric crowd was already spent. The Canadian singer's easygoing pop didn't stand a chance.

With only a few weeks to find and break in two core members of his six-member band, Bruce and Appel placed a Musicians Wanted ad in *The Village Voice* and vowed to give all comers a full thirty minutes to show what they could do. The sheer number of applicants turned the process into a marathon, which would require more than the week or so of time they had secured for the process at the Studio Instrument Rentals rehearsal space. That would cost money, as would the salaries for the band members and the crew they needed to move the gear and keep it functioning. Bruce made it clear that he didn't want to take the band back out until the new players were chosen and adequately prepared, but every time Appel ran the numbers on their next month or two he couldn't make it work. Feeling pushed to the brink, the manager wrote a memo and distributed it to Bruce and everyone else on the scene so they would know where they stood and what risks they would encounter if they didn't get back on the road, and soon.

Titled "THE REFERENDUM ON WHETHER OR NOT BRUCE SPRINGSTEEN AND THE E STREET BAND SHOULD

PLAY THEIR SCHEDULED ENGAGEMENTS OR NOT," the single-spaced memo presented twelve numbered arguments for performing the next month of shows. The litany started with the $2,000-a-week nut they had to meet to run the auditions. "At this rate we will last one week and a half longer," Appel wrote, implying that the band's coffers topped out at $3,000. And the group had other bills coming due. "Clarence Clemons will be tarred and feathered by the Internal Revenue Service next Monday," he continued. They needed to buy new amplifiers and other gear, plus continue paying salaries for the weeks Bruce wanted to spend getting the new musicians up to speed, and where was that money going to come from?

From the manager's desk it all added up to disaster, and not just for their immediate economic health. "Cancelling all these gigs could give Bruce Springsteen & the E Street Band a bad reputation," he went on. "No artist can stand up for long with a reputation for cancelling gigs." They'd already taken time off over the summer: "We've only worked 20 nights out of a possible 123 in the last four months." The arguments went on and on, each less refutable than the last. They needed to build up a cash reserve to help fund tour legs reaching into the West, the deep South, and other regions they'd never played. Which they would need to do if they wanted to win new fans in those areas and inspire them to head to their local record shops and start buying Bruce Springsteen records. "We'll never reach the charts unless we work," the manager wrote. "CBS has taken the single that we worked on for three months, to be frank, lightly." Worse, the company had already advanced the money to make their next record, and if they weren't making progress on the album, while also not playing shows, the executives would start to wonder what the hell they were up to. And speaking of people they were about to aggravate, don't forget agent Sam McKeith and his bosses at the William Morris Agency, whose time and resources had been invested in securing all the bookings they were about to cancel.

Appel offered a simple solution: they should ask Sancious and

Carter to put their new band on hold for the next six weeks so they could play the scheduled shows with Bruce and the band. Certainly they could use the salary money, Appel reasoned. And if that didn't convince the departing musicians, they could make sure Sancious knew that the $500 they still owed him for his work on *The Wild, the Innocent* would be in his pocket a lot sooner if he did his part to make sure the band could keep working even as they auditioned replacements: "If they work with us for a month or a month and a half more we all prosper by the move." Appel signed off, "I humbly submit this for your consideration."

Bruce considered his manager's arguments, shrugged, and said he wanted to cancel the shows anyway. He had his reasons, too: In the end it would be far more efficient to make sure they hired the right guys and prepared them to play their songs in the right way, which would also prepare them to work on recording the next album. End of discussion. Appel swallowed hard and said okay, he'd figure it out. He knew of only one pool of money he hadn't tapped yet, and so he went to the bank that held his children's college savings accounts and took every penny.

Max Weinberg saw everything he needed to know in the ad that ran in *The Village Voice*'s Musicians Wanted classified column on August 8, 1974. A band was looking to add some players. A pianist who could cover everything from classical pieces to Jerry Lee Lewis. A trumpet player who could play R & B, Latin, and jazz. They were also looking for a violinist, but because Weinberg played the drums his eye was drawn to the first line.

"Drummer (no Jr. Ginger Bakers, must encompass R & B and jazz)."

The explicit call for simplicity, emphasized by the request for a pianist capable of handling the old-school rock 'n' roll represented by Jerry Lee Lewis, piqued Weinberg's curiosity. He called the number on the listing and scheduled an audition. Only sixty other drummers were in line ahead of him.

The auditions were a grind, but in the end the final choices were easy to make. Weinberg, who showed up with only a bass drum, a snare, and a hi-hat plus a show drummer's ability to read and respond instantly to a bandleader's visual cues, won the drummer's chair. Roy Bittan, a classically trained pianist with years of rock band experience, took over Sancious's spot.

The new lineup was billed for the first time as Bruce Springsteen and the E Street Band, a name that won out over the Duke Street Kings and the Incredible Jersey Jukers. The reconstituted band debuted at a pair of what they called open rehearsals at the Main Point nightclub in Bryn Mawr, Pennsylvania, on September 19. From there Bruce and the band went back on the road, playing a couple of college dates before returning to New York for a high-profile show at the Avery Fisher Hall in Lincoln Center on October 4. Performing for a capacity audience in the formal hall, Bruce and the band, with Louis Lahav's wife, Suki, joining on a few songs on violin, played an impassioned yet celebratory show, unspooling almost every song from *The Wild, the Innocent,* half of *Greetings,* some choice soul covers (including the rarely played Sam Cooke hit "Cupid"), and, tucked in the middle of the set, two new songs, "Jungleland" and then the debut of "She's the One," a slam-bam rocker about a hot but elusive woman who, as Bruce sang, *burns just like the sun.*

"She's the One" was still in development, and when Weinberg first heard a tape of the song it was set to the sort of country funk that reminded him of the Band's "Up on Cripple Creek." But the heat in the song put the drummer in mind of the bop-bop-bop-BOP-BOP rhythm Bo Diddley introduced to American soul and pop music in the 1950s. Bruce liked that rhythmic approach so much he both applied it to the song and also made it the point of a long, jokey introduction of the tune, warning that this next one was set to a beat "that makes the good girls go bad and makes the bad girls get worse." Which might not have been true, but a whole night of rock 'n' roll rhythm proved too much for Avery Fisher's adjustable stage, whose hydraulic front end started collapsing during the encores. "I can't remember what song we were playing, but the front end of my piano, and Bruce's microphone, were on the part that went up and down," Bittan says. "And I'm looking forward and I can see the front's starting to descend. I have no idea if someone hit a button by mistake or if it was an electrical glitch. All I know is that it was one of those moments where you go, *This can't possibly be happening.* Bruce just picked up his microphone and took a step back to the part of the stage that wasn't moving. And I just sat there and thought, *Is my piano going to crush somebody in the front?*" Happily, the stage kept its legs beneath it for the rest of the encores, and when the last echoes of "Quarter to Three" faded everyone went home in one piece.

When Bruce started sketching ideas in the first half of 1974, his plans for his third album had projected only a modest step beyond the two records he released in 1973. The nine titles listed on the first tentative song list he made for the album included four songs that he had considered for earlier albums: "Architect Angel" and "Visitation at Fort Horn" were first recorded around the sessions for *Greetings* in 1972. Of the other songs, "Janey Needs a Shooter" had been around since 1972 and "Thundercrack" was at least partially recorded for *The Wild, the Innocent*. Less is known about "Two Hearts" and "Here She Comes," while "Angel Baby" and "Glory Road" were either early versions of songs that wound up on the new album or simply contained words, phrases, and melodic twists Bruce would strip out and use in "Born to Run," "Backstreets," and "She's the One." Of all the songs on that original list, only "Jungleland" would survive in recognizable form.

The next song list dusted off another old one, "Song for Orphans," and added new titles, or placeholder names, including "Harlem," "Blondie," and, in a nod to the sound and feel he was increasingly drawn to pursue, "Elvis Style." Another song list from 1974 added titles, including "Wild Billy's Song to Orphans" (sounding like a retread of two separate songs); "Street Fight"; "Shootout in Chinatown"; "Born to Win"; "Baby & Me (Blondie)," almost certainly a new iteration of the earlier listing of "Blondie"; "Orbison—Born to Be Alone"; and "Lonely Night at the Beach," along with "Jungleland" and, finally, "Born to Run." Also listed was a new song Bruce wrote down as "Jr. Walker Groove—A Love So Fine."

It's hard to tell if Bruce's lists were intended to describe his plans for the album or if they're just songs he was working on at the moment. Most of the titles on the early list don't seem to have found their way into a recording studio, but one song that did served as the focus of the band's first recording session with its new members on October 16, 1974. It was an evening session at 914, where they took a stab at a song Bruce was calling "A Night Like This." The song's music and most of its lyrics would remain but he revised its name repeatedly in the next few months, first to "A Love So Fine" and then eventually to "So Young and in Love." But at this session the climactic line in the chorus, and thus the title of the song, was "A Night Like This."

The tune is straight out of the Asbury bars, a full-tilt rock 'n' roll song built on solid drums and galloping bass, over which the piano and organ present dueling fills, the sax squalls, and Bruce's vocal describes another wild night on the shore, where *the rat trap's filled with soul crusaders / They're all bopping and popping and jumping to Little Melvin and the Invaders,* a shout-out to the soul band Tallent played in (with Clemons guesting on occasion) before landing in Bruce's scene. That the song's title, and central line in the chorus, had just changed becomes obvious on the session tapes when Bruce sings the wrong words in one attempt, dropping *A love so fine* for the original *A night like this,* just before the whole take fell apart. He laughed it off, and his high spirits continued when he called the band and everyone else present into the studio to help perform the mill, the theatrical term for the sort of party noises—whooping, hollering, singing along—he wanted for the song's backing. "Do the new men know what a mill is?" he asked just before the take, his mouth audibly full. "I'll mill with a mouth full of oatmeal cookies!" Another voice chimed in: "Will this get a credit on the album?"

The future of Bruce's recording career kept coming back to "Born to Run," the song they'd spent so much of their time and energy working on, trying to get it so perfect, so overwhelmingly powerful, that not even the most dispassionate Columbia executive could deny it or fail to take Bruce as seriously as he deserved. Bruce could hear the power of what they'd done; he knew they'd produced a recording that was light-years beyond what they'd achieved with their first two albums, that should revise all of the executives' expectations of who Bruce Springsteen was and what he could achieve.

But Steve Popovich had only given it the most cursory listen, while conducting three telephone conversations, and if Koppelman or any of his minions had given it even that much consideration they hadn't let Appel know about it. They certainly weren't going to release it as a single, despite the manager's certainty that the move would work wonders for Bruce's career, get him on the radio, get more people into his shows, prime the pump for a truly massive third album. But Columbia's top executives didn't care.

Convinced that "Born to Run" represented a huge step toward alleviating the company's doubts, Appel figured the time had come to take his campaign beyond the record company's executive floor. The execs wouldn't like it. They might be enraged. Who bootlegs their own artist before the company releases their record? Nobody ever, is who. But nobody ever had an artist like Bruce Springsteen, and Appel wasn't just going to sit quietly while those dipshits smothered his baby in its crib. The manager went to his office, took out a pen and paper, and made a list of all the radio disc jockeys who'd played Bruce's records, who'd had him on the air and/or attended his shows and/or professed their adoration for him and his music. He arranged to make several dozen duplicates of the "Born to Run" master tape and wrote a cover letter for radio programmers and disc jockeys so they knew exactly what it was and why they had been chosen to play the song on their air. The manager figured they'd kick it off in Philadelphia at the start of November, when they were slated to play the Tower Theater. Bruce was scheduled to go on the air with WMMR-FM's Ed Sciaky, one of his biggest supporters. When they got there, Appel handed the disc jockey a tape of "Born to Run" and invited him to put it on the air. Sciaky debuted the song that night, then put it on the station's regular playlist.

And when word of the new song sifted across town and then to other Bruce-friendly stations in other cities, other stations got in touch asking for their own copies and Appel happily sent them out, to stations in Chicago, Boston, Austin, Phoenix, and dozens of other cities. "We had stations all over the country," Appel says. "Primary, secondary, tertiary markets, it didn't matter, we had the nation covered. And then I called up some of my other buddies. 'Hey, you're gonna love this song!'" Appel sent them tapes, and they began to air "Born to Run" too. Then he began to hear from the Columbia executive floor, whose occupants wanted to know what the fuck Appel thought he was doing, but he was happy to weather the abuse. Now, at last, they were ready to listen.

Photograph © Eric Meola

Chapter 10

The Poets Around Here Don't Write Nothing at All

When the Columbia Records executives finally got back to Appel about "Born to Run" in the fall of 1974 the response was essentially positive. They liked the song, they liked the guitar riff, they liked what they could hear of Bruce's vocal. But there was so much music on the thing. It sounded so *dense:* the acoustic piano, the electric piano, the organ, the synthesizer, the glockenspiel, the saxophone, the electric and acoustic guitars, the strings and backing vocals layered so thickly atop the bass and drums that even Bruce's stage-steeled voice couldn't cut through the noise. "I guess it wasn't an easy song to absorb when you first heard it," Bruce says. "Now people have heard it a thousand times, so it all sounds perfectly natural, right? But at first people said it sounded noisy."

All too aware of the precariousness of his standing with the company, Bruce and Appel did not want to come off as inflexible. "So we went into some local Columbia studio in New York one night and we tried to remix it. But we couldn't even get close."

The problem, he says, stemmed from both the complexity of the recording—so many instruments on so many tracks—and the relatively primitive technology of the era. In the days before digital equipment allowed a single technician to manipulate each note on dozens of tracks with the push of a button, the analog recording consoles of the 1970s were controlled by faders, one for each track, that had to be manipulated by hand as the music played. So if you wanted to raise the volume of the saxophone for a particular phrase, you had to have at least one hand ready to elevate that track for however long, while another hand lowered another instrument or vocal track to make room. Then the sax would need to fade down again, and the vocal, or other featured instrument, would have to be elevated. And since the voices and instruments shift constantly in most recordings (the casual listener might not notice, particularly if it's a good mix), the mixing required a lot of hands poised on a lot of faders, all to get a sound that captures a feeling that is, at best, elusive. "No two mixes could ever be alike," Bruce continues. "Particularly in a song with seventy-two tracks of information on, I don't even know, maybe sixteen tracks of tape."

They worked deep into the night before they finally realized that the original mix, the one they'd put together the previous summer, was the only one that captured the essential fear, dread, awe, and excitement that animated "Born to Run." They trashed the new attempts at a mix and stuck with what they had. But it wouldn't be the last time work on the new music dragged deep into the night, only to deliver them to a dead end.

January 1975. It was late in the evening, the clock hands circling toward midnight, and Bruce and the band were in 914 Sound Studios, their usual recording headquarters in Blauvelt, New York. Mike Appel led the session from behind the board, with the engineer Louis Lahav at his side and a scattering of staff, friends, and other hangers-on lurking here and there. The filmmaker Barry Rebo was there too, trying to be as unobtrusive as possible as he kept to the edges, following the action with a video camera on his shoulder. There was tension in the air, but it had nothing to do with Rebo or the gaping lens of his camera.

The thing was, they couldn't get a good drum sound. Max Weinberg sat at his set, thwacking his floor tom, while Lahav fiddled with his dials, stalked into the studio to unplug, replug, and then just physically move the microphone closer to the set, then to the side, and then farther away. But the drum sound wasn't nearly as dismaying as the studio's piano, which kept slipping out of tune. They took a break for dinner and called for the piano tuner, a squat middle-aged fellow who smoked a cigarette while he sat at the keyboard and spun his tuning lever, striking the keys, bending the sound this way and that. The musicians ate with plastic forks out of sectioned Styrofoam boxes while making small talk about movies; Woody Allen's spoof adaptation of *Everything You Always Wanted to Know About Sex (But Were Afraid to Ask)*, some classic film starring John Garfield whose title they couldn't remember, and then, because someone had brought a balloon in for them to bop around the studio, the arty French children's film *The Red Balloon*. This inspired a vivid performance of the film's sole bit of dialogue, the little boy's cries of *"Ballon! Ballon!"* as he chases his runaway magical balloon through the streets of Paris.

When the tuner finished on the studio floor he took Appel aside and explained the real problem: The piano's soundboard is cracked, he said, and wouldn't hold a tuning for more than half an hour, no matter what he did. He was happy to stick around all night, but he'd need to be paid ten dollars an hour throughout. Appel nodded, said thanks, but sent him away. Turning to someone else, he explained his reasoning: they couldn't afford to add someone else to the night's payroll. "Just don't tell Bruce, okay?"

Speak of the devil, Bruce swung through the studio door, saw the tuner packing up, and called back into the control room: "Let's do another take! Roy!"

Back in the studio, the musicians filed in, picked up their instruments, and tuned up. Bruce, in jeans, a T-shirt, and a leather jacket, shouldered his guitar and launched into a jam built around a simple twelve-bar blues, firing off some solos, making room for Clemons to honk along. They went around a couple of times before Appel's voice boomed over the intercom: "Let's get back to 'Jungleland'!"

Fifty years later Bruce regards the song with a kind of awed detachment. Standing in front of the fireplace, poking at the embers, he can't quite say where "Jungleland" came from, or how it found its eventual form. "I wrote 'Jungleland' on the piano in West End Court in Long Branch," he says. "I don't remember a whole lot about writing it. It must have taken a while. I don't know where the lyrics came from, except that was the style I was writing in those days. *The Rangers had a homecoming in Harlem . . .* , I was just writing in this operatic, somewhat Broadway-esque style. Rock 'n' roll images, outsider characters. I was just doing my own thing." He heads back to his chair, sits down, shrugs. "It's just one of those things that come out of you. You don't know where it is, you don't know how it came out of you, and you'll never do it again."

The song appeared to Bruce in the early months of 1974. "Jungleland" came as a kind of expansion on the world he'd envisioned for *The Wild, the Innocent*'s "Incident on 57th Street," with two young lovers navigating the city's cruel blocks in search of some form of deliverance, or perhaps just a few moments of peace. In this new version, the star-crossed lovers are the Magic Rat and a barefoot girl he finds hanging out with a gang of outlaws called the Rangers somewhere in Harlem. Together they climb into his car and head down Flamingo Lane, trailing a line of lit-up police cars bent on bringing the lovers down. The reason for the officers' fury is unstated, except as the latest skirmish in a war between authority and the young outsiders who gather themselves into gangs and rock bands. The distinction between the street fighters and the musicians vanishes in the reflected light of the night in this early version, where *kids flash guitars just like bayonets, hustling for the record machine . . . [they] face off against each other out in the street down in Jungleland.* Whether they're hustling to spin their favorite songs on the jukebox or to build new lives in the music business—which you might also think of as the record machine—is indefinite.

This blurring of the line between street gangs and rock bands, the interchangeability of instruments made for the musician's stage and for the warrior's battlefield, is deliberate and meaningful. It speaks to not just Bruce's understanding of compelling images but also his sense of being under siege as he struggled to maintain his control over his music in a rough and unforgiving business. He was, quite literally, hustling for the record machine, chased down the roads of his imagination by squad cars full of disapproving executives, sirens blaring and guns trained on his back. *Boys flash guitars like bayonets and rip holes in their jeans,* he wrote in one early version, where the cops set off a laser show that lights up the sky and, in his words, *rip[s] this holy night.* He would eventually revise the lyrics, but the urban setting, and the tangled skeins of excitement, awe, and dread, were set.

He was less sure about the piece's musical backdrop. The first verses unspooled over a simple I-V-IV progression, one of the most fundamental sets of chord changes in folk and pop music, each verse ending with a brief upward progression that climbed back to the root chord in time for the next set of lines. The narrative set the scene, the kids hanging around waiting for something to happen, and introduced the couple at the center of the story, then put them in motion before giving way to an instrumental section. The backing gained volume and intensity while Clemons blared over the top, riffing over the verse chords until a sudden pivot sent the music into a new key and an entirely new chord pattern. It's the music that would eventually backdrop the finished song's aching saxophone solo. Now a searing guitar line held forth, but only briefly before giving way to an elegantly swinging piano and sax, as if the song had walked off the street and into a smoky jazz club. More instruments joined and together they picked up momentum until it resembled the rampaging solo section in "Kitty's Back," but again, the music screeched to a halt, the pianist tickling a quick bluesy run that swept the other musicians aside. A few beats of silence, then Bruce started singing, alone but for the piano, describing the street as *a classic death waltz / Between flesh and fantasy*. Another verse played over the familiar chords, the band now behind him, back where the song began. Here the Magic Rat returned. The Rat chased his dream into a subway tunnel, moments before a train came roaring through. The girl assumed the worst and headed home to bed, but then the story took another turn. The Rat reappeared, alive and well on Flamingo Lane, just as the girl reappeared, and they walked off together, vanishing together into Jungleland.

A happy ending, of sorts. And a whole new frontier in the band's musical eclecticism. They started performing the piece during the summer of 1974, and audiences seemed enraptured while they played it, even if the applause at the end was closer to respectful than ecstatic. Certainly, elements of "Jungleland" were working. Bruce just had to pull them apart and see if he could figure out how to put them back together in a way that made both musical and narrative sense. What he didn't realize, back in mid-1974, was that the paroxysm his band was about to endure, the loss of its pianist and drummer, would transform his group, tighten his sound, and, with surprising speed, clarify his vision for the new album, and "Jungleland" in particular.

On that night in January 1975 at 914 Sound Studios in Blauvelt, it had been five months since the Bottom Line performance, and "Jungleland" had evolved significantly. The jazz club digression was gone, and the second instrumental section had been moved to the second half of the tune, where it set the stage for the song's new, far more powerful conclusion.

In the studio, Lahav sat at the mixing desk trying to get a fresh level for Tallent's bass, and Weinberg's drums still didn't sound right, so he went back to thumping the floor tom, thump, thump, thump, thump. Then there was more jamming, the central riff of Elvis Presley's "Burning Love," then the chorus of "The Hustle." Then, finally, they got back to "Jungleland." Bruce led a quick run-through of a sticky part, then the whole band played through the first couple of verses, getting the rhythm back into their bones before finally trying a fresh take. It started with the song's new instrumental introduction. What had once been a simple piano prelude had been revised into an elaborately orchestrated Spanish-style piece, with dramatic violin flourishes, rattling castanets, and booming drums that, for the thirty seconds it lasted, sounded like the prologue to a bullfight.

Bruce listened in the control room, thoughtfully eating Junior Mints until the take broke down again, and they went back to worrying over the drum sound. "Max, hit the tom-tom," Appel said. This went on for a bit, then the band started in again, playing the instrumental part that built to the final verse until Lahav interrupted them so he could do something to the balance. Then Bruce looked up and gestured with a drumstick. "Right now there's not enough sound," he said. "There's no roundness in the tone . . . I don't get . . ." He waved his hands, reclining on the sofa in the control room, collapsed on his side. Finally he shrugged. "Should we let everyone take a break?"

It continued like this for some time. Hours on end. The musical breakdowns, the progress lost for want of a fuller drum sound or of chord inversions that would eliminate the most painfully out-of-tune notes on the already-slipping piano, or because the engineer cut in when he thought the rhythm section rushed the verse. Are engineers supposed to have opinions about the band's feel? They finally got a decent instrumental take, but Bruce, now standing in the vocal booth, told Appel he wanted to try another. Headphones clamped over his ears, eyes shut, he swayed to the rhythm and tried to disappear into his lyrics, determined to breathe life into the most emotionally and narratively complex song he'd ever written. Rebo, his video camera just beyond the glass of the vocal booth, shot in close-up until the take broke down and Bruce, opening his eyes, realized for the first time how closely he was being observed. "Umm, Barry," he said, gently but firmly. "You can't be doing this when I'm doing this."

They started again, stopped again, started again. Even five decades later, it's hard to watch. But for Jon Landau, invited by Bruce to come and observe, the scene at 914 was shocking. "That was murder," he says. "Bruce suggested that I come around as a friend to watch, and it was terrible. Just murder."

Landau had only produced two albums and a few other recording sessions, but he'd done them in professional studios and had been to enough sessions with other artists to know how it was supposed to work. "In a good studio there is a technician on the premises so [an out-of-tune piano] doesn't stop your session, the guy can adjust it very quickly." Toss in the sensitive electronic equipment in the control room, also prone to breaking down, and the perpetual problems with the room's resonance and how it seemed to evade all their attempts to get the right drum sound. "They couldn't get any momentum going," Landau says.

Chatting with piano player Roy Bittan outside the studio as the hours tilted toward dawn, the journalist was reminded that the building they were spending the night in had originally been a gas station, only recently converted to its new purpose. The pianist had played recording sessions with other artists before, and he knew the dynamics of a more professional operation. He could only shrug while Landau shook his head. "What the fuck," Landau wondered aloud, "are we doing here?"

Chapter 11

Wings for Wheels

They had been cultivating their friendship through the summer and fall of 1974. At first it was mostly on the telephone; Bruce would call Landau, or Landau would call him, and they'd talk for hours. About music, their favorite records, the great shows they'd seen, which drummers they thought were the best, on and on. They were both big movie buffs, so that conversation could go on for hours, Bruce enthusing over his favorite classic films, the great John Ford westerns, all the shadowy film noir movies of the 1950s. He had a visceral feel for movies; he knew what touched him. As with everything, Landau went at it in a more intellectual fashion. He'd made a study of both film and film criticism and become a vociferous advocate for the American auteur filmmakers of the 1970s. His analyses of filmmaking and the dynamics of visual storytelling transformed Bruce's grasp not just of that form but also of his own writing, which took on a far more cinematic scope.

Bruce invited Landau to come down and hang out at his place in early winter, but the day they had set for the visit turned out to coincide with a snowstorm that closed the roads between New York and the Jersey Shore. Landau called to suggest they hold off until the snow had receded enough for the buses to run, but when he heard the disappointment in his friend's voice he thought again. The trains were still operating, so the writer bundled up, hiked to the train station, and started a painfully slow journey to Long Branch, New Jersey.

It took five hours to make what should have been an hour-long trip. But when the tall, bespectacled Landau finally arrived at the tiny bungalow Bruce rented on West End Court, the evening got rolling. They dug through Bruce's record collection, spinning their favorites and breaking down what made them so wonderful: how the great Philly soul songwriting team Gamble and Huff structured their songs for maximum power, the way Dion's drummer changes the beat in the bridge of "The Wanderer," how the hi-hat disappears in the chorus of Neil Young's "Cinnamon Girl," that kind of stuff. Near midnight they walked around the corner to the Inkwell Coffee House for a strawberry dessert Bruce liked, then went back to the house and talked until breakfast time, when they returned to the Inkwell for more strawberries. Then back to Bruce's for more talk until midmorning, when Landau ran out of gas and Bruce walked him to the corner where he could catch a bus back to New York.

Bruce stuck with him while he waited for the bus and told his friend how significant the corner, and the bus stop, had become to him. It was the precise spot where he had started his journey to the city the day of his audition with John Hammond at Columbia. A life-changing trip, and now Landau was making the same journey. "It sounds pretty bland, but it was a bonding event," Landau says of that snowy night. "Then I started coming down more regularly."

Soon Bruce invited Landau to come down and sit in while he and the band rehearsed his new songs.

Appel found a vacant warehouse on Heck Avenue in Neptune, just a few minutes south of Asbury, to use as a rehearsal space. They spent most of January woodshedding, working on Bruce's new songs. They also developed arrangements for some old rock songs—the Johnny Rivers hit "Mountain of Love," Chuck Berry's "Back in the USA," Jackie DeShannon's "Needles and Pins"—to tuck into the live set. Suki Lahav joined in to add violin to a striking arrangement of "Incident on 57th Street" and a slowed-down cover of Bob Dylan's "I Want You." Suki also contributed parts to two of the new songs, most prominently "Jungleland," whose introduction had been revised again, trading the eruptive Spanish tango feel for something quieter and more melodic, as if the listener were slipping out of the darkness to encounter the scene about to unfold. They spent quite a bit of time on an even newer song, an upbeat jumble of a tune that pointed in a promising direction, even if it wasn't quite streamlined enough to get there yet.

Bruce's title for the song, "Wings for Wheels," was drawn from the narrator's promise that if his girl drives away with him he'll make her dreams come true. *Well, tonight we're gonna find out how it feels,* he sang. *I'm gonna trade in your wings for some wheels.* The lyrics struck many of the same notes as "Born to Run," from the car-driving narrator to the dream girl he hopes to get in his passenger seat to the transcendence he can sense waiting for them down the road. This iteration was lighter on its feet, more hopeful than desperate. *We're gonna ride all the way to the promised land,* he promises. *I'm gonna dance all the way, dance all the way.* He paused for a sax solo, then leaped back in, the narrator talking faster and faster as he goes, his words rattling out with more verve than care. *Well, I don't know but I've been told / There's something waiting for us down that dirty road,* he says. He brags on his car, an Oldsmobile 442 that, presumably like its owner, has taken its hits but is still hard to beat. Then the highway stacks up with clichés: the summer's over and it's getting cold; the guy and his girl will go to a sandy beach where they'll never get old; he's going to lay the stars at the girl's feet; the 442 is so desperate to leave that its engine is about to overheat. By the last verse even he knows he's gone sailing over the top: *Ah but baby you know that's just jive,* he admits, then throws out even more of the same: *But tonight's bustin' open and I'm alive!* As the song gallumphs to its climax, the narrator ends on another boast—*It's a town full of losers, and baby I was born to win*—kicking off a dance party instrumental, all honking sax and full-tilt boogie, before shifting abruptly to a reprise of the saxophone-led theme that served as the midsong break.

At first Bruce had assumed his third album would be an extension of the sound of *The Wild, the Innocent and the E Street Shuffle* and the songs that had emerged around the same time, extended jams like "Thundercrack" or the revised "Blinded by the Light" they'd started playing, stretched to more than ten minutes by a funk vamp and long solos.

"That was my style, right?" Bruce says with a chuckle. "Eclectic, R & B, stream of consciousness, right? So I wrote the original version of 'Thunder Road' in that vein."

In the first months of 1974 the approach made sense. Between David Sancious, Danny Federici, Clarence Clemons, and Bruce, the band was packed with instrumentalists who could improvise at length, riffing off each other, elaborating on the song until it stretched into something entirely new. "I don't believe in having a band where [the other guys are] just scraping away behind me," Bruce told an interviewer after a particularly hot show in Phoenix in the spring of 1974. "I want 'em to be happening. I got a bunch of guys who play great, let 'em out there. Let 'em play."

When David Sancious was in the band he pulled Bruce in a more experimental direction, not just in the length and breadth of the solos ("We were a jam band," Bruce says, shaking his head while listening to the ten-minute "Blinded by the Light" from the Nashville '74 show) but also in how the pianist's tastes inspired Bruce to add avant-garde touches like the jazz digression he tucked into the early arrangements of "Jungleland." Sancious's extended solo preamble to "New York City Serenade" both highlighted the pianist's artistry and added dimension to Bruce's musical presence. With Sancious in the band, it made perfect sense to lean further into that kind of eclecticism. But three months after Bruce was enthusing about them in Phoenix, Sancious and Carter were gone. Roy Bittan and Max Weinberg took their places, and as the band changed so did Bruce's sense of the album they were about to make together.

They kicked off the winter touring season at the Main Point in Bryn Mawr, performing an expansive eighteen-song set that began with the stripped-down "Incident on 57th Street" before Bruce brought out the full band for a spirited "Mountain of Love" and then a steamrolling performance of "Born to Run," which would have already been familiar to Ed Sciaky's listeners on WMMR-FM. Bruce salted the rest of the show with the new songs they'd been working on in Neptune: "Jungleland," of course, "Wings for Wheels," "She's the One," and the wild, woolly "A Love So Fine," the wannabe bar band classic, which had migrated into the encores. The show concluded with a rambunctious version of "Back in the USA," the lesser-known Chuck Berry number that celebrated the nation through the eyes of an adolescent, home from an overseas journey and ecstatic to be back in the land of drive-in movie theaters, jukeboxes, hamburgers, and the highways stretching off into every horizon. It was an unexpected note to strike, particularly in the cynical mid-1970s, when so much of rock 'n' roll existed in opposition to the sort of youthful naïveté that "Back in the USA" described. But Bruce heard something else: another step in the cultural evolution that led to Bob Dylan and, not too many steps later, to the album he was already struggling to make.

Landau had relocated from Boston to New York City and came down to the shore as often as his work schedule would allow that winter, spending time with Bruce in his bungalow in Long Branch and accompanying him to the band rehearsals in the warehouse in Neptune. Back at the house Bruce would sit at the piano and play him the songs he'd been writing, virtually all of them composed on the instrument's yellowed keys. Writing on the piano altered the texture of Bruce's music and also inspired him to introduce the songs with instrumental preludes that, as with "Jungleland," established the song's feel before the start of the first verse. Bruce would preview his songs for Landau on the spinet, asking for his friend's thoughts on how the songs were constructed and what he might do to strengthen them.

Bruce had always kept a tight grasp on his songwriting. Apart from Mike Appel he hadn't ever asked for, let alone taken, advice on how his songs should be structured. And though Appel had plenty of opinions on the subject, the manager limited his feedback to general thoughts based on what his years in the industry had taught him: that Bruce would need to shorten his songs if he wanted them to get onto the radio; that he needed to leave more space between the words if he wanted his melodies to hit home with listeners. Given Appel's aggressive posture toward every other person on the planet, his deference to his client's authorial impulses signaled his admiration for Bruce's artistry. His highest purpose as his manager, Appel believed, was to serve as a battering ram, opening doors and clearing nonbelievers out of the way.

But while Jon Landau shared Appel's awe for Bruce's abilities, the critic had no trouble telling his friend when he thought a song fell short and what he might want to do to bring it up to a higher standard. Bruce took his thoughts seriously.

"I don't trust anybody, you know, but Jon and I struck up a relationship and I said, 'Well, this guy is theoretically going to be our producer,'" Bruce says, fifty years later.

It's uncertain whether Bruce mentioned to Landau that he was considering adding him to the production team the musician now made with Appel or if Landau imagined that might be a possibility. But the critic had made his passion for Bruce's work obvious, and not just in his criticism. Bruce's respect for his friend's writing, along with Landau's insights into the music they both loved, was just as plain. And when he asked Landau what he thought about "Wings for Wheels," Landau didn't hold back.

The song's problems seemed plain to him when he heard Bruce

playing through it with the band in the warehouse in Neptune. Landau's instincts pointed him toward directness and brevity, toward the songwriter making their point and getting out with a minimum of meandering and repetition. As he still likes to point out, all but two of the songs on the record he produced for the MC5 come in at less than 2:30, and the entire eleven-song album lasts just a few ticks beyond twenty-eight minutes.

That Bruce possessed a more expansive vision than the protopunk revolutionaries from Detroit was obvious to Landau, but so was the disorder within "Wings for Wheels." The music was all over the place, with too much going on instrumentally throughout and a midsong saxophone break that not only interrupted the flow of the lyrics but also popped up again as the second of two instrumental sections after the final verse.

Landau had taken notes as he listened, then ran down the song part by part with suggestions: cut this, get rid of that, move the sax solo from the middle to the end, cut the dance party that comes just after the final verse. Bruce took all his suggestions, and the changes sliced two minutes from the song. Landau also had some suggestions for the final verse, calling for a rhythmic shift and a pivot to a minor chord in order to build the narrative tension before Bruce got to the exultant release of his revised final line: *It's a town full of losers / And I'm pulling out of here to win.*

Landau's suggestions for "Wings for Wheels" not just resulted in the structural changes he had called for but also prompted Bruce to rewrite the lyrics and change the title to "Thunder Road." And once he'd done that, he realized the revised song had altered his sense of the album he was trying to make and the band he had pulled together to make it.

"Suddenly we had a very different album," Bruce says. "We had a very different group sound, and we had streamlined ourselves into not a rock and soul band, but into a tight little five-piece streamlined rock 'n' roll band."

Chapter 12

The E Street Dance

Landau was at home in his apartment one night that winter when the telephone rang. He picked up to hear Bruce shouting excitedly on the other end. "Jon! Jon! What are you doing? Just listen to this!"

He was calling from the warehouse in Neptune; the band was arrayed around him, instruments at the ready. Landau heard him count off a song and heard the quick intro, Bittan, Tallent, and Weinberg swinging gently on three chords descending to a crack of the snare that kicked off a jaunty R & B groove. Then Bruce was singing, right into the mouthpiece of the phone.

Tear drops on the city / Bad Scooter searchin' for a groove / Seem like the whole world walkin pretty / But you can't find the room you need to move . . .

It was a brand-new song, written since the last time Bruce and Landau had been together a few days before.

Bruce didn't bother mentioning the title, but when the chorus came around it was easy to tell what it was going to be: "Tenth Avenue Freeze-Out."

"And it was all there," Landau says, though Bruce would polish the lyrics a bit later. "It sounded great, and he was so fucking excited."

So many of the new songs were rooted in fear. The desperation fueling "Born to Run," the assertion of faith in "Thunder Road," the deadly consequences closing in on "Jungleland"'s Magic Rat and barefoot girl. Even the eroticism in "She's the One" is shot through with danger. But while "Tenth Avenue Freeze-Out" treads the same dangerous streets—early versions of the lyrics described some bad guys from Chinatown coming in to blow the local dudes down; the bridge section lingers over a single line, *I'm all alone,* then concludes with an even more bereft, *And I can't go home—* the groove is so buoyant that the narrator's fate is never in doubt. He's got an ace up his sleeve and, more important, a friend by his side. And best of all, the two of them have a band behind them, moving and grooving with soulful élan.

The words to the final verse weren't quite finished. But the music was so alive, and so full of feeling, there was no mistaking what the unwritten lyrics would convey: friendship, joy, and the power brought to bear when people come together and feel their hearts beating in the same rhythm. *I'm gonna sit back right easy and laugh,* was how Bruce would eventually describe it, *when Scooter and the Big Man bust this city in half.*

The whole thing played like a goof, the sinister faces in the shadows swept aside by the power of Scooter and the Big Man's mighty rock 'n' roll. But the implications of the story, and the fairly obvious fact that Scooter and the Big Man were nicknames Bruce had given himself and Clarence Clemons, invested the song with an autobiographical subtext that made it as real and urgent as any of the others.

Spring 1969.

When Douglas and Adele Springsteen packed up their belongings, their meager savings, and their youngest child and quit Freehold for a new life in California, they left their nineteen-year-old son in an empty house. There were two paid-up months remaining on the lease; Bruce could have lived there alone, puzzling through his future without distraction or disturbance. But solitude was not what he was after. A few days later a car pulled up and out piled Vini Lopez and Danny Federici, the drummer and keyboardist in his band Steel Mill, suitcases and instruments and all, and a different kind of family took residence in the house on South Street. It wasn't what you'd call a domesticated scene; like Bruce, Lopez and Federici were adolescent males with standards of cleanliness and cuisine that ran to the feral. But the music they made together, and the way their individual skills added up to something more than any of them could achieve on their own, created a bond as strong as the one connecting real brothers.

Bruce first felt that connection when he joined the Castiles when he was fifteen. They were a neighborhood band, one of the millions that came together following the Beatles' epochal appearance on *The Ed Sullivan Show* in February 1964. And while the British foursome's look and charisma were every bit as overpowering as their music, the connection between the four musicians, and the way each of them added something unique to the band's chemistry, was nearly as resonant as their music. At least, that's how it felt to a lot of the young men who were compelled to take up instruments and chase the same kind of glory. For a kid who didn't play sports or fit in with the popular crowd in school, joining a band was like joining a street gang for kids who didn't like to fight. It was the family you chose to be in, made up of people who actually shared your interests. And it wasn't a bad way to meet girls, either.

To Bruce all of these things were essential. So while the vast majority of teenage bands came and went within a few months, the Castiles hung together for more than three years, even surviving its members' high school graduation. By then, the Castiles were on borrowed time and officially broke apart during the summer of 1968. Bruce, who had served as the band's lead guitarist and rarely got a chance to sing leads, was already exploring a side career as a solo singer-songwriter. Heavily influenced by Bob Dylan, Leonard Cohen, and Tim Buckley, he started performing his own songs in coffee houses around Monmouth County in the summer of 1968. But Bruce still didn't see himself as a solo artist. By the start of the fall he formed Earth, a power trio that mostly performed songs made famous by the likes of Cream and the Jimi Hendrix Experience. Bruce disbanded the group a few months later when he met Lopez and Federici and joined the band that would eventually be called Steel Mill. That group stuck together for two years, then Bruce formed his most ambitious band yet, a ten-piece rock-and-soul outfit with horns and backup singers modeled after the mini-orchestras fronted by Joe Cocker and Van Morrison. The name of the new combo, the Bruce Springsteen Band, revealed his centrality in the operation. But as he put more focus on his songwriting he felt increasingly torn between the joys of group collaboration and the restless, endlessly evolving needs of his creative muse.

The Bruce Springsteen Band debuted as a ten-piece in July 1971 and played a handful of shows that summer and fall, shedding members as they went. By the end of the fall they were playing regularly, but in small clubs to often indifferent audiences. Introduced to a professional manager in New York, Bruce came to the meeting armed with the singer-songwriter material he'd been developing without his band. "I just thought what I was doing on my own was more interesting. There was more of an original voice in it," he says. He played the same songs when Mike Appel, now his manager, took him to audition at Columbia Records. What they heard impressed them enough to sign him to a three-album deal. At the height of the singer-songwriter era, when Bob Dylan was the reigning visionary and the likes of James Taylor, Jackson Browne, and Joni Mitchell regularly sent their records into the upper reaches of the sales charts, they knew what they had. Or they thought they did, anyway.

When they started work on his first album, Bruce had to talk Appel into letting him use the musicians he'd already played with around the Jersey Shore to flesh out the songs. The production, by Appel and his partner, Jim Cretecos, emphasized Bruce's acoustic guitar—his electric guitar could only be heard on one of the songs—and when he prepared to promote the record in live shows, Bruce had to persuade his manager to let him perform with a band. Bruce called in Federici and Lopez, along with the Bruce Springsteen Band bassist Garry Tallent. Pianist/keyboardist David Sancious, another member of the most recent band, opted at first to stick with a jazz fusion band he had put together down in Richmond, Virginia—he'd be back eventually. The band's newest addition was Clarence Clemons, a saxophonist Bruce met when he jammed with the Bruce Springsteen Band at Asbury's Student Prince nightclub late one night in the fall of 1971. The onstage feeling between Bruce and Clemons was powerful enough to spark a friendship, and from the first night they hung out together, the saxophone player helping to introduce the until-recently-teetotal younger musician to the sacramental powers of alcohol, they forged a bond that would carry them through the next forty years. When Bruce invited him to join his band, Clemons quit the group he was in and declared himself available.

Appel was surprised by how strong a bandleader Bruce turned out to be when he finally saw them play together on the first night of their opening tour. "Mike did not know that that was something I could do," Bruce says. "I remember the first night he said, 'Hey, you know what you're doing!'"

Bruce and his band, as yet unnamed, played their first shows in the later weeks of 1972, then picked up speed in January when *Greetings from Asbury Park, NJ* appeared in record stores. Like the album, the early shows were divided sharply between the songs Bruce performed on his own with his acoustic guitar and the ones that featured the entire band. His ability as a performer shone through both halves, but audiences and critics seemed much more fired up by the sound Bruce made with his bandmates. "He puts all of himself on the line and the images that drop so leadenly off the album cover [lyric sheet] take wing," wrote *Village Voice* critic Dan Nooger after a show at New York's Max's Kansas City nightclub. "If he doesn't get lost under the attendant hype, Springsteen might even do something really amazing one of these days."

Starting work on his second album in mid-1973, Bruce felt increasingly drawn to the sound and feeling of his work with the band. Sancious returned to the fold that spring, and the added dimension afforded by the dual keyboardists gave their performances that much more power.

It also inspired Bruce to write songs that allowed his musicians to flex their skills, as on the rampaging jazz-rock tune "Kitty's Back" and the more rocking "Thundercrack," both of which served in large part as delivery systems for the instrumentalists' extended soloing.

All along, Bruce had been reflecting on the communion that took place during shows, not just between the musicians, in that holy collaborative friendship / gang membership, but also between the band and the audience and within the crowd itself, all the people coming together to escape the grind of school, work, of fitting into some preordained role in traditional society.

This vision led to "The E Street Shuffle," the tune that served as part of the new record's title track as well as its spiritual headwaters. It all came down to that magic moment when the lights went down, the music kicked off, and the entire scene lifted off of the ground. Or, as Bruce put it: *The teenage tramps in skintight pants do the E Street dance and everything's all right.*

Though Bruce wrote and performed it initially as a full-speed rave-up, "The E Street Shuffle" later evolved into something slower and silkier, a love song he almost always prefaced with an elaborate shaggy dog story about the night he first encountered Clemons in Asbury Park. As he described it, the saxophonist appeared to him as a fearsome presence: a large African American man coming out of a stormy night in a silk suit, apparently impervious to the elements. Confronted by the big man, Bruce at first assumes he's about to be mugged and tosses his money onto the ground. Instead, Clemons holds out a hand. Bruce reaches out to take it and when they touch . . . this was when Bruce started singing . . . *sparks light on E Street when the boy prophets walk it handsome and hot . . .*

The rest of the songs on *The Wild, the Innocent* describe the crucial role of the band, now including prodigal pianist Sancious, in less direct, yet even more vivid, ways. In the way Federici's accordion lends so much grace to the ballad "4th of July, Asbury Park (Sandy)." In the easy way the piano intro travels through the classical, blues, and jazz idioms to set up the acoustic-guitar-led verses of "New York City Serenade." Federici, this time on organ, takes a lead role in "Kitty's Back," and the entire band navigates the hairpin turns of "Rosalita" with such ease it's tempting to think of it as a simple rock 'n' roll tune, when it's anything but. And when Bruce uncorks his joyous boast—*The record company, Rosie, just gave me a big advance!*—it's the rising notes of Clemons's saxophone, with the entire band surging just behind him, that gives his crowing such resounding authority.

They finished recording *The Wild, the Innocent and the E Street Shuffle* at the end of September 1973, and when the time came to present it to the newly appointed A & R head Charlie Koppelman, Bruce went by himself. *Greetings,* his first Columbia album, released eight months earlier, had not fared well, so there was renewed hope placed on this new recording. Whether Koppelman had heard the record before their meeting, or if this was the executive's first listen, is ambiguous. However it happened, he wasn't impressed.

"He wanted me to record with studio musicians in Studio B or something on West Fifty-Seventh," Bruce says. Once he reworked the songs in Columbia's own studios, with the pros who played on so many of the label's hits, Koppelman said, the album would be smoother and more professional, just the sort of thing they could get onto mainstream radio stations all across the country.

At first Bruce just stared back at him. "I think I just said, 'Well, this is my band, and this is my record.'" Koppelman shrugged, said okay, and that was that. The executive wasn't going to force Bruce to change his record. But he also wasn't going to invest much in promoting an album that didn't sound like something he thought would sell.

"He may have been having a bad day, but there was nothing we could do about it," Bruce continues. "The record came out and went right into the trash."

Koppelman's promise to declare Bruce's second album dead on arrival was not made lightly. *The Wild, the Innocent and the E Street Shuffle* was released on November 5, 1973, to next to no fanfare from Columbia Records. If Bruce had started 1973 as one of the company's most celebrated new artists, he ended it as something more like an afterthought. The release was attended by no ads in the trade papers, or anywhere else. If any of Columbia's promotion representatives tried to talk up the record to radio station programmers or record store owners they did it on their own, not as part of a company-wide campaign. When Bruce and the band went to record stores in the cities they visited on the road they rarely found copies of *The Wild, the Innocent* or *Greetings* in the racks. The shop owners they talked to, along with some radio personnel at the stations that invited Bruce in for interviews, started telling them about a curious phenomenon. When Columbia reps saw copies of Bruce's albums they grabbed them and offered to replace them with copies of the latest record by another young Columbia artist. *Piano Man* was breaking onto playlists on FM radio stations around the country, and listener requests, along with sales, were on the way up. So was Billy Joel. Bruce Springsteen, on the other hand, wasn't going anywhere.

Except Bruce didn't see it that way. And even if he had his fears, and the occasional dark night of the soul, he also had his music. And, just as important, his band. And when they were playing, and whoever had come to see them was in the room, his doubts evaporated and, just like he said, sparks lit on E Street.

Chapter 13

Magic in the Night

The recording sessions picked up at 914 Sound Studios for a night in February with an attempt at the song Bruce was calling "Wings for Wheels." The tune that would soon evolve into "Thunder Road" was still in its shaggier, *The Wild, the Innocent*–style form, the verses leading to instrumental sections that segued into other verses, which led to different instrumental sections before a boogying climax that might have matched the feeling of the lyrics, but they were awfully shaggy, too. Once Landau made his case for revising the song, Bruce called a halt to the recording. He took his friend's suggestions for simplifying the song's structure, then rewrote the lyrics to excise the post-adolescent silliness and give his narrator's words a kind of gritty poetry.

Paired with music balanced between taut and elegiac, the lyric begins with the narrator standing outside his beloved's house. Mary's got music playing and comes out dancing, but the song she's listening to is Roy Orbison's 1960 hit "Only the Lonely," a strikingly sentimental and archaic reference for the mid-1970s. The narrator isn't concerned with time or style; he's after something far more meaningful than youth or beauty. *Show a little faith, there's magic in the night,* he declares, and the song takes off. "Thunder Road" describes nearly the same situation and proposition that animates "Born to Run." The singer is stuck in a nowhere town he's desperate to escape and urges a woman to join his getaway. But unlike the car-focused narrator of the other song, the nameless singer of "Thunder Road" both understands and has empathy for his woman's internal struggle. He knows of the heartbreak she's endured at the hands of other men; he knows she's been waiting for some heroic figure to sweep her up and carry her off. And while he's as battered by life, and his car is something less than the chrome-wheeled, fuel-injected hot rods racing on the circuit, his heart, and intentions, are pure. *Come take my hand,* he urges.

Once again, the road the singer yearns to travel doesn't lead to a particular destination. He talks about the promised land, about some kind of heaven waiting on the other end of the tracks. Again, the most important part of the journey is choosing to go. To make the leap that transforms a gauzy daydream into reality: *To trade in these wings on some wheels.* But if Bruce stripped most of "Born to Run"'s original gothic imagery from that song, he sets "Thunder Road"'s final verse in a cemetery of adolescent fantasies. Here the cars are burned-out skeletons; the boys drift like ghosts, their spirits done in by Mary's rejection of their affections. All they can see of her now is the remnant of her graduation gown, lying in shreds on the side of the road. He warns that if she stays she'll be a ghost too, which is why our narrator is already behind the wheel, holding the door open. *We're riding out tonight to case the promised land.*

A crucial moment in "Thunder Road" comes about two-thirds of the way through the lyric, when the narrator throws open the car door. It's the first explicit sign that the song is as much about its author's life as it is about the blue-collar friends, neighbors, and strangers whose struggles he's witnessed throughout his life.

"Every character you write is an alter ego," he says now. But when the young man in "Thunder Road" shows up at Mary's house with his fully loaded car, he arrives with a musical instrument tucked into the back seat. And this, he says, is what holds the key to his future.

Well I got this guitar / And I learned how to make it talk.

For Bruce, who had been so focused on music as an adolescent he'd put off learning how to drive until he was well into his twenties, the vehicle that mattered the most came with six strings. And now that he was down to his last shot at redemption, as a Columbia Records artist, at any rate, he needed to make sure the road ahead was as clear as possible.

Sitting with Roy Bittan outside the 914 studios that night in January, Landau asked the pianist about the recording he'd done in his pre–E Street days. Had he worked in any of the New York studios? And if so, did he know of one that would be suited for the sound Bruce was trying to achieve for his new album? Bittan had only been in a few recording studios, but the best, by far, had been the New York City outpost of the Record Plant, near Times Square on West Forty-Fourth Street. It was a newer place, had a good warren of studio suites, and had been the central recording location for John Lennon's most recent albums.

Armed with that information, Landau approached Bruce a few days later. "You're a first-class artist," Landau said. "You need to work in a first-class studio." He'd made a few inquiries, he knew of a place that could work: the Record Plant, in midtown Manhattan. Bruce called Mike Appel and asked him to make it happen, no matter the additional expense. Appel did so immediately. Bruce and the band played a few more shows in early March, then Appel cleared the schedule for the duration. The musicians spent a week or two recharging their batteries while Bruce continued to polish the songs, with more editorial consults from Landau.

With recording sessions booked to start in mid-April, Bruce

rang Appel with another instruction. Bruce's first two albums had been coproduced by Appel's songwriting and management partner, Jimmy Cretecos. Worn down by the months of financial hardship, Cretecos had left their co-owned business in early 1974. Bruce stepped in to coproduce the "Born to Run" single and would stay in that role for the rest of the project. But when they got started at the Record Plant he wanted an additional chair set in front of the recording console. From this point forward Jon Landau would be joining them as the album's third coproducer.

If Appel registered a problem with Landau's new role, it was strictly financial. They were already in debt to Columbia for Bruce's first two albums (recording advances were applied to the artist's account as debt against subsequent sales, and artists whose albums didn't sell accrued significant deficits with their companies; by early 1975 Bruce's account at Columbia was in the red to the tune of something like $300,000). Record producers typically got a small percentage of their albums' profits, but Appel, as always looking to save a buck, first offered Landau a fee closer to the $150 weekly salary they paid the band members. Landau appealed to Bruce, who told Appel it would never do. Within a few days they worked with Columbia's executives to pitch in to a more generous deal in which Landau would get a more standard 3 percent of the profits.

Appel's willingness to make room for Landau on the project, despite the fact that it would cost him money as well as influence over his one and only client, revealed something of his commitment to Bruce. The artist had other dedicated acolytes—including Peter Philbin, who moved from Los Angeles to New York and pursued a job at Columbia Records in order to be a part of the scene, and Louis Lahav, who risked his growing career as a recording engineer in order to mix sound and do whatever odd jobs needed doing (driving the van, carrying luggage, etc.) when his wife, Suki, started playing violin with the band on the road. Neither they nor any of Bruce's other foot soldiers could match Appel's dedication, nor his sacrifice for the cause. He'd quit his salaried songwriting job to become Bruce's comanager and coproducer, then worked for next to no money, running up debt on his credit cards to keep the band on the road and then dodging bill collectors when they figured out he couldn't pay, and even draining his own kids' college savings account to help keep the operation afloat. Appel's belief in his client's artistry was so profound he would gladly say and do the most outrageous things to gain him the attention he was sure he deserved, even if it meant alienating industry figures who could be useful to him personally.

So if Bruce really felt like Landau could help push the new album over the top, Appel could only do what he could to make it happen.

"Mike wasn't obsessively territorial about those things," Bruce says. "He went along with Jon coming in as producer. He went along with us moving the studio. If I wanted it and needed it and felt it was important, he was in it with me."

Columbia had more complex reasoning for agreeing to contribute to Landau's payment for working on *Born to Run*. Most immediately, the company had already invested in Bruce's career, and a significant percentage of their executives, if not the ones who sat in the larger offices, still believed that he could become a successful, even significant, artist for the company. But more than that, they knew who Jon Landau was. They knew he was an influential critic at some of the nation's largest and most powerful music publications. When he'd published the "rock 'n' roll future" column the previous spring, even the Columbia executives who were the least enthusiastic about Bruce were impressed.

And when word came that Landau was eager to coproduce one of their artists' new album, the executives were delighted. After all, Landau wasn't just a critic. He was also the editor of *Rolling Stone*'s reviews section. His feelings about artists, and perhaps about their record companies, could make the difference in whether the younger generation's leading music / pop culture journal covered an album or an artist. At a moment when *Rolling Stone* was at its most influential, having a highly placed friend at the magazine could only be good for a record company. Coughing up an additional 1 or 2 percent from the potential profits of an album by an artist who had yet to earn a dime for the company, on the off chance that this next one would finally make Springsteen a hit, was an easy call. Of course they'd do it.

Now all they needed was for Bruce, with Jon Landau at his side, to make the album that would turn him from someone who might be rock 'n' roll's future into something more like the biggest rock 'n' roll hero of today.

Chapter 14

Like a Vision

In Bruce's vision the sun has just risen. It's morning, everything is just beginning. He can sense the freshness of the breeze, the chatter of the birds, the pulse of the new day. The opening notes on the piano, three chords descending to a minor, pausing briefly, then hopping upward again to an arpeggiated fourth before repeating, then moving up to trace a higher chord across the upper reaches of the keyboard. The same chords come in a new pattern, gaining momentum as we hear the first notes of the singer's voice. *The screen door slams / Mary's dress sways.* Bruce imagined an audience just settling in. This, he thought, is the invitation.

He already figured "Thunder Road" as the opening song for the album. It was also the first song they worked on when they started sessions at the Record Plant on April 18, 1975.

Once they set to recording basic tracks at the Record Plant, the work went quickly. Bruce and the band had been rehearsing the songs for months, mastering their parts until they could pull them off in their sleep. The process was particularly easy now that Jon Landau, in his new role as coproducer, convinced Bruce to limit the lineup for the original tracks to the band's core members: Max Weinberg on drums, Garry Tallent on bass, Roy Bittan playing piano, and Bruce on guitar and vocal. They saved Clarence Clemons's saxophone solos for later. They also opted to bench organist Danny Federici for the duration of the sessions. This was a result of the emphasis Landau put on musical precision. Federici was a brilliant musician, but his style was almost entirely improvisatory. When Federici put his hands on the keyboard he could only play what he felt in the moment and either couldn't, or wouldn't, replicate a part he'd already played, even if the two performances were scant moments apart. Bittan, on the other hand, had no trouble playing the same part from take to take, so he would play piano during the basic tracking, then overdub an organ part when the time came to go back and flesh out the track.

The first completed takes of "Thunder Road" were captured the second day in the studio, the core of drums, bass, piano, and some light guitar Bruce played while singing a guide vocal over the top. He was still fiddling with the lyrics and still wasn't sure what the woman's name should be. He'd called her Angelina in the "Wings for Wheels" version they performed that winter, then changed it to Chrissie on some early attempts.

At the Record Plant they ran through the song a few times, making adjustments along the way. Bruce's guitar was barely audible, and the feel was off.

"Sounds lousy!" he declared cheerfully after another attempt. "Stiff as a board! We need some reverb."

Turning to his bandmates, he tried to loosen them up. "Play it a little . . . um . . . not quite as much hesitation."

They started again, but it was still tentative. Bruce talk-sang some lines and tried different melodic variations on others. And he still wasn't sure about the name. Chrissie became Christine, then Mary, then Christine again. He was looking for the right feel, the right number of syllables, a name that fell easily across his tongue. Notice how all the names have the same origin and come with the same radiance. The glow of faith.

Oh, oh come take my hand, he sang on an early take. *We're gonna ride all the way to the promised land.*

No wonder the musicians sounded tight; the stakes of this journey were as high as they come. Starting another attempt, Bruce tried again to loosen them up.

"Take eight, don't be late, meet ya at the gate, so don't wait."

They played through it again, then—oops.

"That was so good I broke a string."

Then:

"Take ten, we're gonna do it again!"

Then, finally:

"Adjust your headsets! Fasten your safety belts! Here we go!"

The opening chords played, the sound of the morning sun slanting through the trees, the girl coming through the front door, the journey starting again.

He began to think of the album as a series of linked songs describing a single day in the life of a young guy in central New Jersey, following him through a long day and endless night in which nothing, and everything, happens. But it was also about creation. About all of life, love, joy, pain, and sacrifice. From Freehold to Eden to heaven to hell and, maybe, back again. The connection between Bruce, the characters in the story, and the central protagonist in the New Testament is unstated but clearly implied. Certainly from the perspective of the kid who left his nowhere town to take on the greatest quest he could think of.

"I was concerned about one thing, which was making an absolutely great rock 'n' roll record," he says in 2024, sitting by the fire on his seventy-fifth birthday, thinking back to the early spring of 1975. "Whatever happens after that I don't have control over. But I *do* have an opportunity to make a record. And I want to make the greatest rock 'n' roll, man. I want to make the last rock 'n' roll album you're ever going to need to hear."

He wasn't shy about his ambition back then, either. Which may have had something to do with the stiffness of those first takes, the sheer weight of the burden Bruce and the band were just shifting onto their shoulders.

"I was on a mission," Bruce says, and here, nearly fifty years after he was trying to decide whether to name the "Thunder Road" woman after an angel, the mother of Jesus, or Jesus himself, his language becomes particularly telling. "I gathered my disciples around me and we were *in*. We were going for the throat."

The "Thunder Road" sessions introduced some new faces into the mix. Jimmy Iovine, a twenty-two-year-old recording engineer who had been trained by the Record Plant's owner, Roy Cicala, came straight from spending two years working with John Lennon on his albums *Rock 'n' Roll* and *Walls and Bridges,* and on Harry Nilsson's *Pussy Cats,* which Lennon produced. Originally Iovine was meant to serve as Louis Lahav's assistant engineer, but that arrangement fell apart after one or two days, when a combination of factors (newly fledged coproducer Jon Landau chafed against Lahav's assertiveness; Suki Lahav was impatient to return to Israel) led to the original engineer's departure.

With Lahav out of the picture Landau turned to Iovine: Would he be comfortable serving as chief engineer? Iovine, who was both ambitious and, following his stint working shoulder-to-shoulder with a Beatle, remarkably confident, said of course. Iovine moved into the engineer's chair, making room for his friend Thom Panunzio, another young member of the Record Plant's staff, who stepped in as assistant engineer. Neither of them had any idea what they were getting themselves into.

A telltale problem emerged during the "Thunder Road" sessions, when Bruce couldn't find a guitar sound that fit what he'd been hearing in his head. Or maybe he'd written the song on the piano and then worked with Roy Bittan to create an arrangement that channeled the song's most essential feeling through that instrument. Whatever the case, nothing Bruce did on his Telecaster seemed to fit. On one take the guitar was too loud and kept stepping on Bittan's part. On another attempt he played so sparingly it didn't seem to have any guitar at all—which not only clashed against Bruce's conception of rock 'n' roll but also knocked the legs out from the crucial line about how the narrator had staked his future on his mastery of the instrument: *I got this guitar / And I learned how to make it talk.* Except now the song's arrangement had struck his Telecaster mute.

How could they make it work? Bruce tried everything: play more, play less, turn it up, turn it down, make the tone grittier, make it sweeter. Or all of those things, in various combinations. The work went on for hours, well into the evening, past midnight, pushing toward dawn, with no resolution in sight. "We were in there for, I don't know, twelve hours. And he's just jammed, you know?" Iovine remembers the scene, shaking his head. Bruce hunched over his guitar, fiddling with knobs, voicing the chords one way, then another. That would go on for long stretches with no recording, and at one point young Iovine put his head on the board and fell asleep. He doesn't remember how long he was out. It might have been three hours, it might have been ten minutes. It didn't matter. When Bruce was ready to try another take Iovine was unconscious. Bruce didn't want to wait long enough for the engineer to rouse himself and punch the right buttons. The gig was to be awake, and ready to go, at all times. "He wanted to kill me," Iovine says.

Second engineer, Thom Panunzio, charged with maintaining the technical aspects of the recording process, learned quickly that Bruce had no interest in the physical limits of the recording studio. In those days professional recording consoles offered a finite number of tracks—basically, channels that can capture different instruments and/or performances that are then layered into a finished recording. An artist attempting to weave multiple instruments, vocals, and other sounds would, in those predigital days, often collide against the limitations of the tape and the machinery. But a canny engineer could then blend finished tracks, bouncing, say, half a dozen tracks into one track, thereby freeing five channels for additional layers. The trade-off came in the degeneration of the signal, and the fact that reducing six tracks into one means you can no longer adjust the relative level of the bounced-down tracks. This creates a conundrum for an engineer, who is charged with both maintaining the sonic quality of the recording and making certain the artist's creative vision doesn't collide with the studio's technical restrictions. This was particularly crucial during the *Born to Run* sessions, given the complexity of the arrangements, and Bruce's refusal to acknowledge any obstacle standing between his imagination and reality. "You might get to the point where there were no more tracks, right?" Panunzio says. "Like, 'I'm sorry, we're out of space.' But that meant telling Bruce he couldn't do something, and that didn't work. You had to make it work. That was the job."

Only the music mattered. Every word, note, strum, and shout had to be right because this was *it;* there was no later, only right here, right now, and everyone in the room had to invest their labors with the same sense of mission. "Everything was on the line, right?" Iovine says. "Everything. Because I could tell from my initial impression of him that he didn't want anything else. He didn't want anything that you had, he didn't want anything anybody had. He just wanted to be *great*. And it was so powerful that he made me think like that. I was a kid from Brooklyn, right? I never knew anyone who thought like that. So I'm like, '*Ohhhhh, shit.*'"

If Appel served as the fiercest advocate for Bruce in his struggle with the Columbia executives, radio programmers, and the rest of the music industry, Landau did his part to make sure that everyone in and around the recording studio understood that their assignment included a spiritual commitment to Bruce's vision. One of Iovine's favorite stories about his work with Bruce recounts the night he was, for one reason or another, feeling cranky, stomping around, sighing, being visibly frustrated. He has no idea why he felt that way, but he has a clear memory of how Landau responded. "He took me aside and he said, 'I'm gonna tell you something that you've never heard in your neighborhood, or your parents have never said to you,'" Iovine recalls. "And he said, 'This is not about *you*. This is about the *big picture*.'" Landau's words were a turning point for him, Iovine says, and not just for his work with Springsteen.

And then there were the songs. When he was tapped for the sessions, Iovine had no idea who Bruce was. When he told Panunzio of his new assignment he was convinced the artist's name was Bruce SpringFIELD and it took some doing for Panunzio to convince him otherwise. Whatever, he was a professional, he'd record anyone he was assigned to work with. But then he walked into the studio on the first day and came across Bruce sitting alone at the piano, playing and singing "Thunder Road." Hearing the song for the first time, even with the lyrics still rough in places, sent Iovine reeling. "I was like, 'Oh wow, this is an incredible piece of music,'" he recalls. The way the chords flowed through the verses, the stubborn hope that filigreed the lyric, which erupted into something like triumph in the instrumental coda, sounded nothing like any of the music coming over the airwaves in the mid-1970s. Half a decade removed from the 1960s, in a time of reduced expectations and foreshortened horizons, with his own future severely in doubt, this skinny, bearded kid from blue-collar nowhere pointed into the distance.

It's a town full of losers / And I'm pulling out of here to win.

Chapter 15

All the Wonder It Brings

Once they got into the swing of things at the Record Plant, the work went smoothly. For a while it felt like good fun. They'd start a song, play through it a few times while Landau and Mike Appel listened for the sound and feel and engineers Jimmy Iovine and Thom Panunzio tinkered with the equipment. Once all that was wired down, they'd try to get some takes in the can. When attempts broke down Bruce made a point of keeping the atmosphere light.

"Ladies and gentlemen, this is a song written by my horse," he announced before one attempt at "Thunder Road." "Ready, pardners? Okay, here we go. Pick it up from the sensuous omnipotence. Watch out for your codas. Are you ready?" It started, stumbled, stopped. While the others got ready to try again Bruce, still in a cowboy frame of mind, started playing the riff to "Tumbling Tumbleweeds." "It's the greatest . . . the greatest record ever made," he declared, which must have been a callback to some other joke because he and Appel both cracked up, riotously.

When an attempt at "Jungleland" broke down for an equipment fix, Bruce turned up his guitar and ripped out the opening chords of "Louie Louie." The other musicians jumped in instantly, and they played through a few verses before crashing to a stop. Speaking through the control room intercom, both of Bruce's coproducers weighed in on what they'd just heard.

Landau: "Nothing is better than 'Louie Louie.'"

Appel: "The rudiments of rock."

Landau: "It'll live forever."

Bruce agreed, still standing at his microphone in the studio, and started musing about the simple song's visceral power.

Bruce: "We oughta start doing that, people go nuts for that song. May be one of the ultimate rock songs. And man, people just go crazy." He shook his head in wonder. "We gotta start doing that one."

On other days Bruce steered the band into other rock and soul standards. Fats Domino's "Ain't That a Shame." A deliciously crunchy cover of the Searchers' version of "Needles and Pins," Sam & Dave's "Soothe Me," then, most ecstatically, Link Wray's 1958 instrumental "Rumble." One of the most distinctive instrumentals of the rock era, it snarled and strutted with so much of the good old *fuck you* in that nasty guitar that dozens of radio stations banned the song for fear its rampaging sound would inspire teenagers to riot. "That's the sound!" Bruce crowed as his mighty E chord frayed into feedback. The other musicians leaped in after him and they let it rip together, raw and loud, the window-rattling sound of a rock band cutting loose. He wasn't hearing enough of that these days, and it was beginning to bug him.

The old way, the way they used to do it, had always made sense to Bruce. Starting with the full-band songs on *Greetings from Asbury Park, NJ* and then on every song on *The Wild, the Innocent and the E Street Shuffle,* they had recorded with the same philosophy: put the band in the studio, set up the microphones to capture the sound as clearly as possible, count off the song, and then let 'er rip. They would have worked out live arrangements of the songs by then and would probably have played most of the tunes onstage dozens of times before taking them into the studio. By the time the tape rolled they'd be able to play all the new material with real power and authority. Which didn't explain why the music never sounded quite as overwhelming after it was recorded, mixed, mastered, and then pressed onto vinyl. Landau's original review of *The Wild, the Innocent* had made that point a few months before he met Bruce in Boston in the spring of 1974, declaring the songs brilliant but the production disappointingly anemic. The low end didn't resonate, he complained, and the absence made the music sound hollow. Bruce had taken Landau's words to heart, and when he first called Landau after they met, Bruce quizzed him on what he'd meant and how he thought they might fix the problem. Landau had been happy to talk it over. It made sense to Bruce; that was just the start of their collaboration.

Preparing to launch the sessions at the Record Plant, Landau made his case for moving to an overdub-heavy style of recording. As much as he admired Bruce and the band's live performances, Landau argued that the technical verities of the recording studio created a necessary paradox: capturing the parts separately and then layering them together would result in a recording that sounded more alive and powerful than a full-band-in-the-studio recording ever could. "My mind is very structural and I wanted to simplify everything," Landau says. "I was interested, first and foremost, in the songs. The melody Bruce was writing and the words and the singing. So the way we recorded the album was about the songs. It's about the singing. It's about the album being about Bruce."

Certainly, Bruce wasn't opposed to having his songs, and his vocals, serve as the focus of the sessions. He had made a point of getting signed as a solo artist and relished his control over the material and the band's performances. But he also had strong ideas about how rock 'n' roll was supposed to be played and how it should sound. And that was the sound of "Louie Louie," "Rumble," and all the other bar band classics he and his bandmates had ripped out between their painstaking attempts to make recordings of the new songs that sounded more live than a live performance. "Everybody said Bruce live was better than the records he had made, and we just had to capture him live in the studio. But the way we made the record was the exact opposite of what you'd think to do, because *Born to Run* is a studio album, and it sounds like a studio album," Landau says. To his ears this was a distinct improvement. Bruce, on the other hand, had his doubts. "There were conflicts," Landau says. "But I think he was in conflict about everything."

Other factors upped the pressure, too. The executives at Columbia were already talking about getting the record out by the end of the summer. Every hour they spent tinkering on some micro-detail added to the risk that they'd miss that deadline. And if they blew that, there was no telling what the Columbia executives would say, other than goodbye.

It had something to do with the immediacy. With visceral impact. The feeling you get from being on the line, waiting for the countdown, and then stomping on the accelerator. In Asbury Park the hot-rodders lived it on the Ocean Avenue / Kingsley Street circuit while the rock 'n' rollers chased their own kind of glory in the nightclubs alongside the seaside loop. Bruce knew where he belonged, but he could sense what the drivers were after, and when he noticed one of them hanging around at the Stone Pony, Bruce started talking to him.

"He was an interesting young guy," Bruce says now. "He was always at the Pony, so I got to know him a little." One night the racer took Bruce out to see his car. It was pristine: he lived out of town, and on weekend nights he'd bring the car to Asbury on the back of a trailer, not letting the tires touch asphalt until he was close to the action. Bruce drove with him a time or two, learning about the racing scene from the passenger seat. Like a lot of competitive drivers, the racer had a day job, doing what he had to do to support himself and keep his car tuned up and full of gas.

But what mattered in his life was what happened when he was behind the wheel, circling Ocean and Kingsley, keeping an eye out for other fast cars, waiting for someone to rev their engine. They'd circle each other in that way, showing off what they had under the hood, talking up their own power and speed, then throwing down the challenge: wanna race? Terms set, they'd head out of town, the two competitors and a legion of friends, followers, and street-racing fans, to a straight piece of highway they could use as a drag strip and get in position before the cops could get there. The revving would rattle your sternum. Then came the countdown and the blast of the engines, the scream of rubber, the high-beams shining like spotlights in the dark, salty air.

Bruce's infatuation with the racers began well before he climbed into that one guy's passenger seat. They were still airing out songs at 914 Sound Studios in the fall of 1974 when he first took a stab at the song he originally called "The Night." It didn't have lyrics at first, but it was easy to sense the Asbury circuit in its sound. It opened at full blast, Weinberg machine-gunning the snare, Bruce's strumming hand matching the drummer beat for beat, his other hand chording near the top of the neck for maybe two beats, then zooming down for two more, then zoom, the rest of the band leaped in, Bittan nailing a chord high on the piano keyboard, the bass pulsing fast beneath that and Clemons's saxophone, a force of nature coming at you head-on. "The Night" came and went from Bruce's Album Number 3 song lists that winter, but it kept popping back up. "I don't remember how I wrote it, or even writing it at all," he says now. "I remember playing it for Jon. It's got that great sax intro and really moves. A great little pop song." And in the spring of 1975, as work on *Born to Run* was slipping into the trickier emotional currents, "The Night" felt like good medicine.

At the Record Plant they knocked out the basic recording of "The Night" in one night; the music was that powerful, the construction of the tune so obviously right. This was how he imagined it feeling, the sound and velocity of the cars screaming down a dark and empty highway. In Bruce's memory they had the music wrapped up, overdubs and all, before he figured out the first word of the lyrics. At one point he brought a cassette of the music into the office of Michael Pillot, the promotions executive who was one of his strongest supporters at Columbia, and had him give it a spin. Pillot nodded excitedly when it was done: The first Springsteen instrumental! he said. He'd been hoping for something like this. Bruce just laughed. Oh, it had lyrics . . . he just hadn't finished them yet, he said. Oh well then, better still! Pillot said.

The words he hadn't recorded yet, or the feeling that inspired them, were somewhere in the back of his mind when Bruce, Tallent, Weinberg, and Bittan laid down the basic instrumental track in early May.

And the world is busting at its seams / And you're just a prisoner of your dreams / And it's alright / You work all day to blow 'em away at night.

This was the racer's life, and his too, their quests interweaving in the bars and on the streets that ran alongside the Asbury boardwalk. They all spent their days waiting for the sun to fall. The hours of preparation, hood raised, head and hands deep in the guts of the engine, making sure everything was just so. Then the circuitous journey to the racing spot, one eye out for the cops as the time approached. The taut moments of waiting, then the countdown, the flashing lights, the sound, and, finally, the speed.

And you're in love with all the wonder it brings / You're an angel with a new set of wings / Hangin' on tight / You work all day to blow 'em away in the night.

Chapter 16

Scooter and the Big Man

Sometimes the most powerful messages come between the words. A joke carries a deadly serious subtext; a photograph of a pair of musicians, one leaning on the other's shoulder, tells us something that should be obvious but keeps getting forgotten. Or maybe it comes even more subtly, in the form of a good-time song about a kid who takes a wrong turn on his way home.

They knocked out the basic track to "Tenth Avenue Freeze-Out" in short order; a tracking session on May 15, then some overdubs to fill in Bruce's vocal, Clemons's saxophone part, and then the horn parts. The brass session would prove to be the most difficult piece of the puzzle, serving ultimately as both an illustration of the production's problems and then a turning point in the album, the makeup of the band, and the evolution of Bruce's artistry. But what made the song such a crucial part of the new album was how it straddled so many lines. How it propelled a classic rhythm & blues groove into the now; how its narrator alluded to the racial and class divides of modern America so clearly and yet breezily, and how his connection to his band, and particularly to the African American saxophone player he referred to here, and evermore, as the Big Man, granted him the power to transcend it all.

The title phrase is poetic nonsense. What's a Tenth Avenue freeze-out? As Bruce has said, he has no fuckin' idea what it means or where it came from. Seemingly from the corner of his imagination that produces images that bypass the brain and head straight for the gut. When Bad Scooter, the name our narrator takes, sketches the dark urban street he finds himself on, tiptoeing in the shadows he hopes will shield him from the scary locals, you know exactly what a freeze-out is, and why it's necessary to steer clear of any street whose residents are likely to bring one down upon a lonesome stranger wandering into their midst.

And I'm all alone, I'm on my own / And kid, you better get the picture . . . / And I can't go home.

Oh, but Scooter has an ace up his sleeve.

Well, everyone was singin' when the Big Man joined the band / Coastline to the city all the little pretties raised their hand . . .

The early lyrics he sang for the guide vocal on the basic track broke down there; Bruce barked something fast about the Big Man bringin' it up and the heavy hitters givin' it up, something like that. What he was after, and would soon achieve, was about the power of unity: between musicians, between friends, between white and Black. Lost and alone on the mythical Tenth Avenue, Bad Scooter is in grievous danger. But once the Big Man joins the band, announcing his arrival with a bluesy blast from his horn, the dudes from Chinatown jump back. Or, as Bruce / Bad Scooter would eventually proclaim:

I'm gonna sit back right easy and laugh / When Scooter and the Big Man bust this city in half / With a Tenth Avenue freeze-out.

When he wasn't recording or working on his songs, Bruce thought about the cover of the album. How he should pose, what he should wear, what it should symbolize.

Some recording artists couldn't care less about album photos and graphics; Bruce wasn't one of them. He brought the original *Greetings from Asbury Park, NJ* postcard he'd found in a boardwalk gift shop to Columbia's chief designer John Berg and talked up its significance so intently that Berg granted an exception to the label's policy of compelling all first-time artists to decorate their debut albums with well-composed headshots. Bruce cared so little about the stamp-sized photo of himself that went on the back cover he let them use a snap someone had taken of him looking like the Dylan-esque urban folkie on a rooftop in New York, and didn't complain when they airbrushed out the skyline and replaced it with a generic ocean backdrop to fit the Jersey Shore theme. The *Wild, the Innocent* cover was a more traditional singer-songwriter headshot; caught in close-up, the artist peers to the left in a moment of deep reflection, forehead puckering, hand draped across his lips. The more distinctive band photo on the back finds the musicians looking raffish in front of an appealingly grungy storefront at the shore, seemingly after a long day on the beach: unbuttoned shirts, faded denims, board shorts, feet bare or in sneakers or flip-flops. What's most noticeable now is how drummer Vini Lopez, towering over the others at the back, looks like the dominant member of the gang. "People kept calling me Bruce after that," he told me in 2010. The actual Bruce was determined to avoid this confusion on his all-important third album. He knew it had to look as distinctive as he was trying to make it sound.

Bruce spent his boyhood in a working-class neighborhood whose population, while largely white, was dotted with the homes of African American families. Institutional racism hung over Freehold like it did, and does, over most of the nation, but Doug and Adele Springsteen had progressive sensibilities and were economically and socially disadvantaged enough to have an immediate sympathy for anyone who had to struggle to pay the bills at the end of the month. Bruce played with Black kids when he was small and took immediate and lasting joy from the work of the great soul / rhythm & blues artists of the 1950s and 1960s. When he started forming bands around Asbury Park in the late 1960s and early 1970s he was quick to team up with the African American keyboardist David Sancious, whose musical brilliance he recognized the moment they first jammed together at the Upstage. Sancious was an important part of his bands during his stints over the next five years, and when Clemons entered the scene with his saxophone, his charismatic presence—by turns sweet and sinister, and always soulful—became transformative. A broad-shouldered ex–football lineman with big musical chops and an innate theatricality, the saxophonist served as Bruce's spiritual anchor and physical protector, mostly onstage, but sometimes in real life, too.

Sancious tells a story about the summer day in 1973 when the racism came for him and Bruce's racially integrated band. They were south of Asbury, probably an hour down the shore, preparing for a show that evening. Given a free afternoon Sancious set out for the beach, found an open patch of sand, rolled out his towel, unpacked his book, and settled down to relax. But that became difficult when he noticed the two young white men sitting a few dozen feet away. Because they were glaring at him, and muttering. That's when it occurred to Sancious that he was the only African American in sight. And that while he had spent his whole life on the Jersey Shore, he'd never met an African American who talked about visiting Long Beach Island, let alone kicking back on the sand. And then the guys weren't just muttering. "They started saying stuff, you know," Sancious recalls. "Weird stuff, and insults, and like, 'What are you doing here?' Calling me names. And it got kind of uncomfortable." Sancious was still a teenager then, slim and bookish. Not what you'd call physically imposing. Neither was Bruce, but he happened by and when he clocked the scene he beelined over and sat next to his pianist. Sancious told him what was up, and after shooting the hostile white guys an icy look, he reached over and picked up a piece of driftwood the size of a small baseball bat. "I was ready to knock those fuckers right over the fucking head," Bruce says now. Which was certainly a brave thought—but in those days Bruce was maybe 140 pounds when dripping wet, standing five feet nine inches, so he didn't make for much of a fearsome presence either, even wielding a chunk of wood.

So it became a stalemate. The two beefy white assholes versus the two skinny musicians. "It was a really ugly scene," Bruce says. "They tiptoed right up to the line, you know, being loud enough so we could hear them. It was one of the ugliest scenes I've seen in my life. You know, just in-your-face racism. Right here on the beach." It seemed like something bad might happen. Then Clarence Clemons came strolling across the sand.

There was a reason Bruce called him the Big Man. The saxophonist was six feet five inches and oversized from his feet to his muscled gut, broad-beam shoulders, and tree-trunk legs. He was also observant. Noticing the aggressive posture of the angry white boys, reflected by the stubborn posture of his typically peaceful bandmates, Clemons strode over and sat down. Sancious, sotto voce, told him what was going on. The muttering, the insults, the air of incipient violence. Only now Sancious had two friends at his side. And the bigger of the two was not in the mood for this kind of shit. First Clemons glared at the white boys. Then he climbed to his feet. Took a step in their direction. "That pretty much shut it down, you know," Bruce says. Because that's when the white boys jumped to their feet, turned in the opposite direction, and scuttled away.

More than fifty years later the memory lingers for Sancious. The unexpected threat, the growing fear, and then the appearance of his bandmates. "I had Bruce on the one side and Clarence Clemons on the other, ready to put a hurt on these fools if they wanted to escalate anything," he says. "I just knew there was nothing bad going to happen to me." That was the point of a band, or this band, anyway. A musical conglomeration you could depend on, on stages large and small and anywhere else the locals might throw down their version of a freeze-out.

Bruce's first idea for the cover of *Born to Run*, back when he was thinking of calling the album *Between Flesh and Fantasy*, contrasted two images, the first showing Bruce in a city street scene in daylight, animating the theme of flesh. The second image, the fantasy, would be set on the mini-golf course next to Madam Marie's fortune-telling booth on the Asbury Park boardwalk, with a full moon lighting the night and Clemons lurking in the background. Bruce had moved on to a new album title by the spring of 1975, and his visual concept changed with it.

The stakes had grown. Instead of making just another rock 'n' roll album, he was determined to make a great one. More than that: *the greatest rock 'n' roll album anyone had ever made.* The songs he'd written, and was still revising so painstakingly, took on the biggest ideas he could imagine. Love and lust. Commitment and betrayal. The comfort of home and the promise of the open road. Innocence and experience. And, as always for a boy raised in the Catholic church: sin and redemption. Ideas that went well beyond the traditional subject matter for the sort of old-school rock 'n' roll he had set out to revive, but that was the point. He was taking up the standard that Elvis, Chuck, Buddy, Bo, and all the other founders had hoisted two decades ago. Repairing the fabric, holding it aloft, and carrying it into the light of the modern world. He was approaching the album as if every chord, every note, and every syllable had to express something important, and he had to take the cover image just as seriously. The clothes, the pose, the expression on his face. All of it had to say something. Had to connect to the past and point the way into the future.

What was it that Jon Landau had written, almost exactly a year ago? *I saw rock and roll future and its name is Bruce Springsteen.* What the cover of *Born to Run* had to make clear, with a single glance, was this: the rock 'n' roll future had arrived.

Eric Meola saw Bruce perform for the first time at Max's Kansas City in 1973, was impressed, then saw a few more shows. He bumped into Bruce on the street in the summer of 1974, and when he went to see another show in Red Bank, New Jersey, a few weeks later Bruce remembered him, and noticed his camera. Meola asked if he'd be willing to pose for some photographs and Bruce said sure. The two met at the shore a couple weeks later, then the photographer showed the images to Mike Appel, who liked them enough to ring Meola when the time came to make some new photographs for the cover of Bruce's third album. Next Bruce called Meola and they began to talk about what the pictures should look like. They both had ideas. The photographer had heard enough of the new music to be struck by some of the images. *Runaway American dream* made an impact. So did *We're riding out tonight to case the promised land*. He thought back to "4th of July, Asbury Park" on the previous album. "It's not girls under the boardwalk," Meola says. "It's *factory* girls."

All of this made Meola imagine the photos in black and white. Bruce quizzed him on this for a bit, then added his own twist: he wanted to pose with his saxophone player, who was, as Meola knew, Black. And this sealed it: a Black man and a white man, wearing black (or dark) and white clothes, posed against a sheer white backdrop, captured on black-and-white film. Contrasting tones, brought together into one image. That, they both decided, would work. They set a date and time for Bruce and Clemons to come to Meola's studio downtown, but then a recording session ran long and they couldn't make it. They set another date and time, and the same thing happened. Now Meola was frustrated—he had other clients and other assignments, damn it—and he told Appel as much. They set another time, 10 a.m. on June 20, and Meola girded himself to be stood up again. Instead, his buzzer went off at precisely 10 a.m. It was Bruce, carrying his guitar and a sack of clothes, and he was accompanied by Clemons, who had his saxophone and an armload of wardrobe options.

Bruce came with a black leather motorcycle jacket he'd gotten from Appel, tight denim jeans, and a white tank top with a deep scoop neck and an artful tear on its left side. Clemons wore black leather pants and had both white and black button-up shirts and an oversized black fedora as a crown. Bruce also brought a hat, a gray corduroy newsboy-style cap, but it didn't read right on film and was mostly cast aside. What became much more central to the photos was the button he'd pinned near the front end of his leather guitar strap. It was a souvenir from the Elvis Presley fan club, NYC chapter, with a vintage headshot bracketed by the words *King's Court* on the right and *Elvis Presley* on the left, both in blue script. Across the top, in bright red, were the words *ELVIS the KING*. Coming at this moment in Presley's career, deep in the karate-kicking, fried-peanut-butter-and-banana-sandwich-gobbling, fistfuls-of-pills-popping era, when the King struck younger listeners as a dismaying vision of everything wrong with the older generations, it was a statement.

They played around with poses for a while, most featuring Bruce and Clemons wielding their instruments in dynamic ways. For a while Meola posed them back-to-back, with Bruce standing on a box to make up for the saxophonist's eight-inch height advantage. They kicked the box aside and stood facing the camera, Bruce in front, with Clemons behind him, fists raised. Meola had Bruce pose alone, hoisting his guitar, showing off his Elvis button, then without his guitar, but with a radio held in the crook of his arm. Bruce had brought a pair of Converse sneakers and they tied them to his guitar's tuning pegs so they dangled—born to *run,* right? They went outside and posed for a few shots on the sidewalk to take advantage of the pattern of light and shadow cast by the fire escape just above. Back in the studio they brought back the box and stood next to one another. After two hours they called it good and left Meola to develop and edit the images.

When Meola delivered the contact sheets of the images to Appel's office, Bruce and his manager looked them over and settled on a shot of Bruce and Clarence posing side by side, the one with Clemons, saxophone to his lips, digging deep to get a mighty blast out of his instrument. Bruce, his guitar strapped over his shoulder and Elvis button in plain view, leaned on his shoulder, face lit by a loving smile. It was a striking, and strikingly beautiful, image. For everything it said about who Bruce was—a dyed-in-the-leather rock 'n' roller, an Elvis fan, a lithe young man who could wear the hell out of a torn tank top—and how much he admired his African American bandmate, on whose shoulder he leaned, both literally and figuratively. That relationship, as complex as any white/Black, employer/employee relationship could be, was also, clearly, founded in a love that both underscored and transcended the fraternity of every rock 'n' roll band.

The beefy boys from down the shore, and all their white supremacist ilk, would hate it. Which was the point. Because here they were again. Scooter and the Big Man gearing up to tear their city in half.

Chapter 17

It's Elephants, Baby!

You could hear the disagreement forming as they prepared to record.

"We're so ready we scare ourselves!" Bruce declared just before a take. It was the seventeenth attempt; they'd already been at it for hours. That take broke down, there was talk of going faster, or slowing down, or adding more reverb to the drums. They started up again, got through a verse or two, before Bruce waved his hand and the music stopped again. "That was too slow," he said. From the control room Mike Appel hit the intercom button. He didn't like it slow. But then, he didn't like it fast, either. But he was being patient, giving his client room to figure this out for himself.

Mike: "It's elephants, baby." This probably wasn't intended as a compliment. But this was the process, you never knew where it was going to lead, so keep moving, keep it going. "*Elephants!* Let's do it on eighteen, slow, slow."

Bruce, laughing: "One time for the elephants!"

It was May 8, 1975. Bruce was in the studio with the core band. Mike Appel sat at the board with Jon Landau on one side and engineer Jimmy Iovine at the other. They were trying to get a basic track for a midtempo ballad Bruce called "Linda, Let Me Be the One," and once again, the right approach seemed to be evading them. It was another one of Bruce's more direct, old-school-inspired tunes, the rhythm drawn from Phil Spector's production of "Be My Baby," the song Spector cowrote for the Ronettes with Jeff Barry and Ellie Greenwich. The music on the verses and chorus was just as straightforward, though the sax break leaped into a different key, then executed a neat climb back to the root chord for the third verse. Still, "Linda" was a relatively flat song compared to everything else they'd been working on, and Appel couldn't hide his disdain. They got a few takes down that first day then moved on to other songs. When they took up "Linda" again on May 19 Landau was leading the session. Bruce was still finishing a snack when he called for the session's first attempt.

Bruce: "Slate the watermelon take!"

Landau: "Watermelon, take one."

Now they were leaning into "Linda"'s rhythm & blues influences. Roy Bittan worked a Fender Rhodes electric piano, which gave his part the sweet chiming sound of a vibraphone. It's a sound familiar from modern soul ballads (think "That's the Way of the World," by Earth, Wind & Fire and Stevie Wonder's "You Are the Sunshine of My Life"), underscoring the frustrated passion in the story. The first verse introduces us to Eddie, a teenage boxer lost in the spell of Linda, who lives with her parents in a town where, we're told, the streets run with tears. Here Bruce's imagination tilts back to the gothic, as Eddie, *an angel in defeat* in Bruce's words, gets pounded in the ring and hits the canvas with only Linda's scarves for comfort. At night he stands guard outside her window and asserts his devotion by carving Linda's name into the upholstery of her father's Cadillac. Her father's response to this gesture is unrecorded. Bruce's voice takes on a sweet, scratchy sound that underscores the tune's bruised romanticism. In the final verse a rainstorm chases Eddie and the other midnight boys into the basement of a Catholic church.

Talking fast cars and chrome parts, different worlds and strange girls / *Empty homes, busted hearts, and kneeling with Linda in the dark.*

Take after take. After a while Bruce and the band started an instrumental jam, Bruce leading the way on the guitar until he waved the other guys off and Landau punched in from the control room. "Play the number," he said, and when Bruce noodled out another riff he hit the mic again. "Send in the next guitar player, please!" There was a moment of silence, then Landau set up the next go-round. "Okay, watermelon take. Take three."

Was Appel even in the room? His voice is absent from the session tapes.

Bruce's manager and coproducer's other least-loved song was "Lonely Night in the Park," a harder-edged tune with lyrics that explored many of "Linda"'s themes, albeit through more grown-up eyes. Here the Freehold-like setting of Eddie and Linda, who live in family homes and hang out in church basements, has evolved into something more like Asbury Park, with its bars, boardwalk, and piers. The role of Eddie is played by Johnny, who falls for a nameless topless dancer from a strip club called Toyland. When she finishes her shift he finds her at the bar and soon they're on the beach together, running through the shadows, falling together on the sand, and sharing a moment of tenderness. It doesn't last. Soon she's gone and Johnny is drinking under the pier with a friend named Kid Blue, who enjoys himself a little too much, grows unwell, and then pukes on Johnny's shoes. Another fun night at the seaside.

With no parents in sight Bruce cranks up his guitar and slashes at the strings, playing a circular pattern with each chord hanging in the air. He belts the lyrics like he's singing a party song, but the party, which we'll recall began at a topless joint, is strikingly joyless. Suddenly it's 3 a.m. and Johnny is alone, walking the streets by himself. *Standing on the corner looking for the light to change,* Bruce sings. *They got nothing left but time.*

They spent a long session trying to get a basic track for "Lonely

Night" in early May, then set it aside for nearly two months. They only got back to it on July 2, when Appel was out of the studio for the long weekend. They fiddled with "Linda, Let Me Be the One" on July 8, but by then Appel's antipathy had apparently taken root. Setting up another take on "Linda," Bruce promised that the next attempt would be "the big one," but his energy was clearly flagging. Girding for another run through "Lonely Night," he geared up by pretending to introduce Black Sabbath, leaning into the microphone to make arena-full-of-screaming-fan sounds. Digging deep for enthusiasm, scraping the bottom of the barrel. Still, Bruce didn't get into the room by giving up when the songs got tricky.

Even five decades later he swears he's going to make a go of "Lonely Night in the Park." "Yeah, that was a good one," he says firmly. "I want to cut that one again."

For his part, Appel still isn't backing down either. "I said, 'Over my dead body!'" he recalls, proudly.

Bruce and Landau felt differently. But Appel was adamant, especially given the other new song Bruce had written. He called it "The Heist" then, though the name would change to "Meeting Across the River." Under either title it sounded like nothing else he'd ever written, closer to modern jazz than rock 'n' roll, centered on augmented chords he arpeggiated on the piano keys to draw out their angular construction. And though he played it for Appel and Landau soon after he wrote it, and Appel told him immediately that it was an incredible piece of work, Bruce couldn't imagine how it could fit on the album they were making. "I still have no idea how I ever wrote those changes, or how I came up with that," he says now.

Speaking from his home in California a few weeks later, Roy Bittan laughs: "I know how!"

One night in the winter of 1975 Bittan went to the Village Vanguard nightclub to see the jazz saxophonist Pharaoh Sanders. A former member of John Coltrane's band, Sanders was a central figure in the free jazz movement of the 1960s. Some of his work edged toward the cacophonous, but he also had some quieter pieces, and something of Sanders's musical palette stuck in the pianist's ear. Visiting Bruce a day or two later, Bittan sat at the piano and when his host went into the kitchen to take a call he started fingering some changes that reminded him of what he'd heard at the Vanguard. "It was just a couple of chords, and I was playing it, and improvising over it, and at some point, Bruce came in and he said, 'What is that?'" Bittan slowed it down and showed him the chords, playing the notes individually. Bruce watched, nodded, and that was that.

A few days later he came into the studio playing a variation on the chords Bittan had shown him, including the note-to-note arpeggiation, with some additional chords and an original melody fleshing out the piece. He'd also come up with a lyric inspired by those B movies he'd been watching, especially the gangster films. Furtive men lurking on the dark end of the street, a beat-up hero with one last chance. Calling it "The Heist" was almost too on the nose—it sounded like a black-and-white flick Robert Mitchum would have swaggered through in 1958. His next title, "Meeting Across the River," left more to the imagination.

Once the music starts it hits you like the first sip of bourbon. Those lean, angled chords cutting through the smoky air. Shut your eyes and you can see it. Over here the piano player slouches in the corner, there a bartender sweeps a rag over the bar. They both look spent, warped by gravity and the years. In another corner two guys hunch over a table, talking about how it's going to go. Bruce had seen enough movies and read enough dime-store novels to get a clear line on the guy's voice. *Tonight's our night, and I know it / It's all set up, and this time we ain't gonna blow it,* he vowed in an early draft. We suspect this might not be true, but we've already seen this movie and the narrator of the song apparently hasn't. Besides, he tells Eddie, to whom the song is addressed, it's a sure thing. All they have to do is get to the city and meet with the guy in charge. He's a fearsome character, they'll want to at least appear to be armed (*Here stuff this in your pocket,* he says. *It'll look like you're carryin a friend*). The third verse moves in closer. He's in dutch with his girl (nameless in the early draft, later dubbed Cherry), because he took her radio to the pawnshop to procure a little operating capital. *Eddie, man, she don't understand / That grand*—later two grand—*is sittin' in my pocket / And tonight's gonna be everything that I said.* He sends Eddie out to borrow a car; the piano slows, then stops. It's hard to imagine this is going to end well.

Every hustler knows the feeling, no matter the hustle. Even from the comfort of his seaside living room, decades after he took the bus into the city to make his stand, Bruce can remember how hot the desperation felt in his chest, and how it came to inform his writing. "I just got into this idea," he says. "This classic sort of underdog guy who's gonna make this score, you know. His girlfriend doesn't believe him, but he's got his wingman, and they're trying to figure it out." He was recalling the day he wrote "Meeting Across the River," but in a sense he was also talking about every protagonist on *Born to Run:* they're all variations of the same guy. The young but battered hero who finds himself held back by someone else's rules, someone else's strictures. Some people might accept it for what it is—the *way* it is—but our hero has a better idea. He'll blaze his own path, thank you very much. He's leaving town. He's taking his car to the races. He's headed to the city. He's hitting the big time.

You need a partner for that kind of operation, a Mary, a Wendy, an Eddie. Bruce's wingman for the last few years had been Appel, and their belief in one another was complete. Appel had quit his job, ditched his other management and production clients, and gone into debt for Bruce, who had signed any and all of Appel's proffered contracts with nary a glance at their contents. And as for hiring a lawyer to look them over . . . well, that wasn't something a Freehold boy would be thinking about. Not this Freehold boy, anyway. If only because the terms of their bond were grounded in something so far beyond the grasp of the law.

"I needed somebody else who was a little crazy in the eyes because that was my approach to it all," Bruce told me in 2011. "It was not business, if business had to be a part of it then it had to be a part of it, but really, it was an idea and an opportunity. And Mike understood that part of it very well."

Landau's heart, mind, and everything else were in it, too. But he'd been to college, then spent years learning about the inner workings of the music industry, from the recording studio to the executive suites. He wasn't personally expert in the intricacies of entertainment law, but he knew enough to know when you wanted to call in an attorney for some backup. Like when someone hands you a contract to sign. Because even if that person is your friend, and even if their belief in you is every bit as fierce as you want to imagine it is, you just want a solid understanding of what you're in for.

Bruce made a mistake by not doing that at first, Landau believed. And now that those original deals were entering their final year, just as Bruce was making the album they all felt would break him wide open, Landau had one piece of advice: get a lawyer to read everything. A big part of Bruce didn't want to hear it: he preferred to work on a handshake and be bound by mutual faith. But he'd grown up a little since he'd signed those deals in 1972. He'd seen some things. He'd met some folks. Had a better idea of how it all worked. And so sure, he'd take his papers to a lawyer. Maybe not immediately, but soon. He wasn't worried, he knew it would be fine. Right? Of course it would.

Photograph © Eric Meola

Chapter 18

And Then You Were the Psychopath

The first tracking session for "Backstreets" came early in the Record Plant sessions. There's an undated reel that seems to be from the first week in April. At that point the lyrics were still unfinished, but the song's emotional landscape was clear. Bruce's thoughts were in Freehold, back when he was a teenager trying to find his way from childhood to adulthood. "It's the loneliness of living like that, with a few friends and relationships maybe," Bruce says. "That's what we were like. We were out at night. We were on our own. It was a different world, you know?" He doesn't explain who the *we* is; the specifics are beside the point.

> *In the basement of St. John's*
> *Where I found her where she fell*
> *Just another wasted sister of a heartbreak hotel*
> *Slow dancing in the dark, oh, bridled to the king*
> *Hopeless as the highway in the freezing rain*
> *That keeps falling on the backstreets*

It was another tune that came to him when he was sitting at the piano. The music was relatively simple, another basic rock 'n' roll progression, four chords looping from a major chord to a minor, visiting the other major chords in the scale, always circling the darker tone. Climbing away in the chorus, but then, inevitably, drawn back in the verses, where the heart of the story resided. The feeling of it arrived unformed. He called it "Virgin Summer" at first, then "Hidin' on the River." He could sense the heat of a feeling, the terrible moment a youngster's innocence is overwhelmed by something bigger and meaner. Teenage memories returned, the church basements and sheltering trees of Freehold, the secret places a lonely adolescent could find refuge. As if anywhere could be safe, as if any friendship was strong enough to survive the wickedness in the world.

From the start the narrator of "Backstreets" was a wounded young man addressing a lost love. In some early versions the friend's name is Chrissie; it eventually became Terry. Given the universe of possible names, the androgyny of *Terry* seems purposeful. When you're a kid getting batted around by your parents, by your teachers, by every authority figure you've ever encountered, any kind of loving relationship feels like deliverance. Even platonic friends can connect with operatic passion. Life becomes a partnership, the bond feels crucial to everything that could and should happen. That's how it felt to the narrator of "Backstreets," who recalls his friendship with Terry in a montage of nighttime scenes that seem to play out in the reflected light of an inferno. A collapsing city, a life in flames. Then comes the story of a friendship, and of friends splintered by a nameless, overwhelming betrayal.

It begins with the story of the friends, told with seething acuity. The narrator and Terry connected in the heat of a summer night and spent their time together navigating the shadows of a cruel town. *Tying faith between our teeth,* he sings, tracing a connection that springs from poisoned ground. *A love so hard and filled with defeat.* The world around them is brutal, but when they found one another they recognized something, and someone, to believe in. And so they set out together, visiting what their crumbling city has to offer. Hanging with the last living members of a legendary street gang near the beach at Stockton's Wing. Crawling through the bars and dance halls in town. Taking inspiration from the glorious characters on the movie screen. *Trying to learn how to walk like heroes we thought we had to be / And after all this time to find we're just like all the rest.* It's that last line that tips the balance. *Just like all the rest.* In a town as corrupt and crumbling as theirs, where even the mighty Duke Street Kings have fallen to ruin, it's a blistering revelation. And it comes just after he's turned to address Terry directly, recalling the night it all came crashing down. *There was nothing left to say,* he says. *But I hated him and I hated you when you went away.* Now he's back in the shadows of the backstreets, alone but for the memory of the nights when he didn't have to be alone. *We swore forever friends,* he recalls bitterly. *On the backstreets until the end.*

One of the things that made Bruce's *Born to Run* songs distinctive was how many of them began with instrumental preambles. Piano-led introductions, mostly, that established the tune's mood and setting. The intro for "Backstreets" is a preview of the verses that builds in volume and intensity until it erupts into the chorus sequence. When Jon Landau started talking to him about editing his songs for maximum efficiency and power, one of the changes Bruce made was to lop the introduction off "Backstreets." Then Landau heard the new arrangement, which began more or less at the start of the opening verse, and ran in waving his hands. *No, no, no,* he cried. *That's a cut too far, you gotta put the intro back in!* Back in it went. And it wouldn't be long before other parts came, went, and sometimes returned. A full string arrangement; a harder guitar sound; grittier, harder-edged vocals; fuller, more romantic vocals. Bruce was up for trying anything, everything.

Circling this way, then that way, until he got dizzy and had no idea where he was standing, which direction he was facing.

Maybe it meant too much to him. When every question feels definitive, every tweak of a knob or sharpening of a tone or slight volume adjustment becomes a matter of spiritual life and death. Lost in overwhelm, gnawed at by doubt, unsure of whom to trust, Bruce got stuck. So he'd go at it like a terrier, circling and circling and circling, almost as if the ceaseless repeated labor was the point of the project. And maybe it was. Because his days felt so torturous. And if you were with him, as in truly committed to him, he needed to know that you could withstand torture too.

"I don't know how to explain this because it sounds like fiction, but Bruce would kill you," says Stephen Appel, Mike's brother and the road manager who also helped coordinate things in the studio. "We're into this project, and we love it. We love him. We love the music. We love the lyrics. We're saying, 'Let's get this great record down on vinyl!' You're working and it sounds great and so you start to think you have it right, but Bruce says, 'Nope, it's shit.' Okay, where do we go from here? And then you work for hours to change it. And then that's done, and Bruce says, 'You know what? Maybe it was better before, because now *this* sounds like shit.' And you would do that for ten to fifteen hours a day." They'd get to the end of the night, probably somewhere close to dawn; try to rest for a few hours; and then be back at it, back in the studio, back under Bruce's warped spell. "And then he would do things to bug you," Stephen continues. "Bruce would go into the studio and play two notes for six hours. He'd tell Jimmy Iovine, you know, 'Hit this! Hit that! Hit this! Hit that, now hit it again!' And it would go on for ten hours, twenty hours, and we're still not getting anywhere, because Bruce *still* hates every single thing he's doing. And that starts to get to you because you keep thinking this is great. And then he brings you down, further down, further down. And then *you* were the psychopath."

When Bruce hears accounts like that he nods, then shrugs. As rough as it was for the others, it was even worse for him. It was terrible, awful, gut-wrenchingly painful. And for reasons he has spent decades trying to uncover, somehow necessary. "That must have been something I needed," he says. "There was a certain amount of self-punishment and self-thrashing for no good reason except for that was the only way I knew how to do it. I didn't know how to do it some other way, so everybody got stuck with it."

What was setting him off? Anything in particular?

"Just life itself, myself, being disappointed in myself, and just, you know, just feeling out of control."

If there was one thing Bruce couldn't tolerate it was that. *Losing control.*

Sometimes the recording sessions fell into silence. The music stuttered and stopped, the thoughts, ideas, and opinions about the music ran out of gas, Bruce would slip away, or perhaps storm off into the studio, find a chair, and . . . sit there. For long stretches of time. Hours, often, when nothing happened. Nothing audible, anyway, because Bruce would be sitting by himself, staring at the wall and saying nothing. Maybe he'd have his notebook at hand. Maybe his guitar was in his lap. It didn't matter. He'd be thinking, maybe trying to figure out something about a lyric or a shard of melody, or the precise texture of a moment of music. Whatever it was, he needed to contemplate it from every conceivable angle, anticipating every potential outcome and conceivable interpretation of that outcome. Or maybe he wasn't thinking about any of those things. "When I get really mad, I get stone-cold silent," he says. "And when I'm stone-cold silent I'm raging, and people just generally stay away from me. Which is probably a good idea."

They had a schedule, and a budget. The Columbia executives were still planning to get the new album out by the end of the summer. And it wasn't like the recording studio came for free. The Record Plant charged premium rates for its time and equipment, and even if Columbia was paying the bills, they were also tallying the amount on Bruce's account with the company: the artist always ends up paying in the long run.

But some things ran so much deeper, and darker, than the music or cost of studio time. Headwaters that bubbled up from between the rocks, poisonous and sweet. The earliest years, when his family lived with his dad's folks and young Bruce assumed his grandparents were his parents and his actual parents were the outsiders. His dad and mom, Doug and Adele Springsteen, moved Bruce and his sister Virginia to another house nearby, but the family connections only became more complicated as he got older. Because Bruce loved his father and, like any young boy, ached to feel loved in return. To feel part of a family, a neighborhood, a community where certain beliefs and truths held strong. These were the things Bruce needed when he was young. And did not receive.

Douglas Springsteen was a large man, from his thickly muscled shoulders to his prominent gut to his powerful thighs. His hair was dark, his eyes like coal, his expression somewhere between distant and absent. And yet he was also a good man. Pulled combat duty in World War II, worked tough jobs when he was well enough, fought his demons as hard as anyone could. It was never a fair fight. They came at him from deep within, held him down and made his days close to intolerable. In the mid-twentieth century, in a blue-collar family where psychiatry was at best an abstract concept, his wife and family had no idea what to think. He veered this way and that; even the smallest tasks could go sideways. Drawing the next breath could seem like an impossible burden. Some nights he slipped outside, got behind the wheel, and drove off alone, drifting through the darkness until close to daybreak.

The old man's disdain got worse when Bruce was a teenager. He was in the Castiles by then, spending most of his weekend evenings playing the hits of the day to other high schoolers at local sock hops and teen clubs. The shows would keep him out late, and when he came home he tried to be quiet, hoping to make it to his bedroom without being noticed. Most often he'd be out of luck. His father would be awake, sitting in the kitchen with the lights out, lit cigarette smoldering in one hand and a can of beer sweating in the other, gazing at something in the darkness.

Doug would sit like that for hours, but when his teenage son came in, guitar in hand and hair bristling over his collar, the old man's eyes would focus and he'd take Bruce's measure. It would start casually enough, the father asking his son where he'd been, what he was up to tomorrow. But he'd be thinking about something else. His own failures, how hard the world could be, what it took to stay afloat, to stay on course when everything else in the universe was determined to knock you sideways. Doug had unique problems. His moods could be wild; some days he couldn't get out of bed, other days he was so high he saw things nobody else could see. And he wanted to steer his son away from his corner of hell. Wanted him to have the foundation, the security, he'd never had. But he had no idea how to say that. He just knew his son was acting like an idiot. Getting lousy grades in school, wasting his time with that goddamn guitar, hanging out with all those other idiots, draped in his moronic clothes and long hair. What was he doing with his life!? *What did he think he was doing?* That part would come out as a shout, his big voice rattling the dishes in the cabinet. Bruce would stand there and absorb it, try not to let it get to him. But he was just a kid, and it hit home. By the time he managed to achieve the safety of his room, he'd feel wrecked.

Everything else would vanish. The hours he'd spent making music with his friends, watching the kids in the crowd move to their rhythm, seeing the girls notice him, hearing their applause when they finished a number, faded to nothing. But he could still hear his father's voice, still feel burned by his condemnation. Even now, six decades later, when he's in his midseventies with fully grown children and, ack, a grandchild, the memory burns.

Blame it on the lies that killed us, blame it on the truth that ran us down / You can blame it all on me, Terry, it don't matter to me now.

Chapter 19

The Heist

Sometimes Bruce and Mike Appel disagreed. As with a father and a son both parties are prone to see things differently from time to time, and when it happens the measure of the relationship is in how they come back together. It comes down to communication, a willingness to try things differently, find a compromise, and also something deeper: trust. And as the sessions stretched on and bogged down, Bruce looked to both Appel and Jon Landau for counsel. And when his coproducers didn't agree he'd have to decide whom to trust. This became particularly challenging when they tried to figure out what to do with "Meeting Across the River."

At first Bruce wasn't convinced it would work on the album. The song he had initially titled "The Heist," with its film noir–style lyric and jazz club music, starring the down-and-outers plotting a score, sounded like the work of a different artist working on a very different kind of record.

The basic track they recorded on May 28, Bruce singing near-final lyrics over Bittan's finely etched piano part, came with relative ease. But as they discussed fleshing out the track with a jazz-trio-style lineup, adding a stand-up bass and a trumpet to riff over the piano and vocal, Bruce and Jon Landau began to drift away from the piece. After all, they had set out to make a great rock 'n' roll album; *the greatest rock album ever!* Every other song on the album hit like an avalanche. But "Meeting" came out of the opposite direction. How could a song featuring a damn *jazz trio* fit in with such an unruly mob? Bruce and Landau didn't think it would. And they had other ideas.

"Linda, Let Me Be the One" and "Lonely Night in the Park" were rock songs that, in Bruce and Landau's estimation, were hooky and pop-friendly. The sort of songs that hit hard but could make it on the radio, too. They'd taken a few runs at both of the songs already, and it wouldn't be that hard to finish them off. Wasn't that the obvious solution to the problem? It sure seemed that way to them. Appel didn't see it that way.

"So they come in, and they say, 'Mike, we know you like that "Meeting Across the River,"'" he recalls. "'We have two songs here. They really have pop appeal.' I said, 'Okay, great. Let's hear it.'" They played what they had on both songs. "So I listened to one and I listened to the other. And I said, '*Those* two fuckin' dogs? You really think those shitty songs can stand next to "Backstreets" and "Thunder Road"? Fuck that!'"

Looking back at it now, Appel still sounds apoplectic. Just because he'd come up through the pop song mills and written lightweight hits for the Partridge Family, it didn't compromise his ability to distinguish between an artistic song that worked and one that sucked. And as the recording ground on through June, with July just around the corner and the late August release date fast on its heels, and as Bruce made certain each session dragged on while he considered, reconsidered, rerecorded, and reconfigured every atom of every song, as the spring slipped into summer, the time for delicacy had passed.

"I said, 'Okay, we haven't finished recording "Meeting." Why don't we focus on that, see where that goes,'" Appel said. "'And then we'll maybe take up these other songs as we go along.' Right. So at least I got them to shut up."

July 2 was slated to be a busy day; they booked the jazz musicians Randy and Michael Brecker, brothers who played trumpet and saxophone, respectively, along with trombonist Wayne Andre. All three were eminent session players around the studios in New York. Randy and Michael also led a popular jazz-fusion band, the Brecker Brothers, so they came with a high profile. Which may have been why Bruce, Appel, and Landau decided to bring them in to track the horns they needed for both "Meeting Across the River" and "Tenth Avenue Freeze-Out." And when Randy got to work on a trumpet part for "Meeting," he quickly proved to be a brilliant addition to the tune. Recorded with reverb and mixed beneath Bruce's vocal, his improvised riffing seemed to be echoing from down the street. Stand-up bassist Richard Davis added an elegant low end, and when they nailed down a final take and listened to the playback it sounded so perfect both Bruce and Landau could no longer remember why the song seemed out of place. "Jon came up to me and sat down and said, 'You were the visionary on this one, Mike,'" Appel says. "Meeting Across the River" would go on the album.

Next, both Brecker brothers, along with trombonist Andre, went into the studio to track the horns for "Tenth Avenue Freeze-Out." And this was where the sessions hit another dead end.

When the horn players arrived at the studio, they went to the music stands that had been set up for them and looked for the arrangement they were expecting to have been written out for them. That was generally how it worked for session players hired to play parts on another artist's tune; either the artist or their producer wrote up parts or they hired a professional arranger to do it for them. That's what the Breckers and Andre were expecting, at any rate. But what they found, in Roy Bittan's handwriting, was a chord chart, an outline of the song's structure. Bruce, Appel, and Landau had assumed the horn players would listen to the track once or twice and work out their own parts, which is a more customary practice in pop and rhythm & blues sessions. What they neglected to consider was that the Breckers and Andre came out of a much more traditional background and had next to no experience writing what pop players called head arrangements. Put on the spot, the horn players did their best to come up with something to fit the song, then set to trying to record it over the existing track.

It didn't work. The parts the horn players had written, defined by stretches of long, hanging notes, sounded a lot like the smooth parts featured on modern pop hits by the likes of Chicago. They lacked the bite and verve of rhythm & blues horns. Bruce, Landau, and Appel tried everything they could think of to make the parts work, running take after take, getting nothing that sounded like the groove they were after. At some point early in the evening Bruce's old friend Steve Van Zandt—they'd met as teenage musicians and Van Zandt served as the second bassist in Steel Mill, then played guitar in the Bruce Springsteen Band and was expecting to stay in the same role when Bruce summoned his band members to play on his first album, but budget constraints had sent him packing—showed up to lend his fellow musician moral support and sat quietly for some time. He switched to the floor after a few hours, then stretched out on his back, legs crossed at the ankles, straw hat perched on his chest. By this point Bruce, dejected, spun around in his chair and gazed down at his friend.

"So what do *you* think," he said.

Van Zandt glanced up and made a face. "I think it sucks."

Bruce grimaced, his face went dark, and he kicked his chair backward, away from his prone friend. "Then you fix it," he snapped. Van Zandt, sitting up, put his hat back on his head, stood up, and walked into the studio. "Okay, boys, throw away those charts," he directed. The Breckers and Andre were taken aback. "He probably didn't know who we were," Randy Brecker says. "He was really, how can I put this, *impolite* about our work." Van Zandt, without even hearing Brecker's recollection, cringes at the memory of his own lack of politesse. "I didn't know they were the greatest horn players in New York," he says sheepishly. Whatever he lacked in his knowledge of the city's first-call horn players, Van Zandt knew quite a bit about arranging horns for rhythm & blues–inspired rock songs. He'd been serving as the manager and producer for his and Bruce's old friend Southside Johnny Lyon and his band the Asbury Jukes, and helped arrange parts for their horn section. He had an intuitive feel for "Tenth Avenue Freeze-Out," and he scripted the horn arrangement in his head on the spot, pointing to each horn player and singing him his part. The musicians scribbled some notes, took up their instruments, and gave it a go.

"And I have to admit, it was way better than what we had going, right?" Brecker says. "They were good lines, and they just fit the tune better. We were done pretty quickly after that."

Listening to the track with the finished horns on top, Bruce went up to Appel and gestured toward Van Zandt. When they were just starting out three years earlier they couldn't afford a second guitarist. Now things had changed. Maybe, Bruce said, the time had come to put Steve on the payroll. There was no maybe about it. Appel nodded and just like that, Van Zandt was back in the band. "It was supposed to be a temporary thing," the guitarist says. "Bruce only had seven cities planned and that was going to be the end. So he said, 'For these last gigs I'd like to front the band a bit. Can you come out?' So I literally joined for those seven shows. And that turned into seven years."

It was becoming an expensive project. All those hours in the studio, the endless takes, the recording and rerecording, the restless pursuit of the right feel, the right tone, a level of polish that would make a track shine without diminishing its hot, angry humanity. As the price scaled higher, word came from the Columbia tower that some of the executives wanted to come in and hear what they'd been up to. Bruce would have nothing to do with that sort of corporate grading session, so he planned to give the executive preview a miss. Appel had no problem stepping up to fend off the suits; he'd been battling those guys for three years already and had at one point or another screamed at them all. Deciding that it'd be best to present the new material with an all-new attitude, they left it to Landau to run the meeting. The coproducer greeted the half-dozen executives warmly, ushered them to seats in the control room. He primed them on what they were about to hear. These weren't final mixes, he cautioned, and some of the songs still lacked solos, vocals, and other finishing touches. But most of the performances were there, and they'd definitely be able to hear the spirit of the thing.

"I was wild about how great this was," Landau remembers. "And nobody was leaving that room without having the Landau experience." He nodded to Iovine and the tape rolled. "Thunder Road," "Tenth Avenue Freeze-Out," "Backstreets," "She's the One," song after song. Heads began to nod, postures eased.

When it was over the vibe was good. Better than good. "They loved it. Whatever reservations they had, financial, whatever it might be, were over. Gone." There were smiles, a little backslapping, then came talk of hard delivery dates, production schedules, release dates. Could they have it ready in time for Labor Day weekend? That became the plan: get us the master by the third week of July, they'd have it in the shops within a month. When the now-cheery executives left the studio, the control room filled with a new realization. Now the abstract talk about late summer had become extremely specific. The time for foot-dragging and fucking around was over.

During a break one late evening Jimmy Iovine headed to the roof to breathe some city air. His hand was on the doorknob, he was about to push through when he heard voices outside. He couldn't make out what they were saying, but he recognized who it was. Appel and Landau. And they were shouting, really having it out. What was the problem? Well, for Iovine it was this: they were both his bosses; he had a good relationship with both of them, and the last place he wanted to be was standing between them when things got ugly. No fool, the young engineer spun around and skipped down the stairs, back to where he came from. Neither Appel nor Landau can remember what they were fighting about. Were there disagreements? To Appel it would have been ridiculous for there not to be. "What, were there three opinionated guys in that room? Yes. And then everything is wonderful forever?" He scoffs. "Yeah, right. Nobody ever says anything that bothers anyone. So that's an unrealistic expectation."

Of course there were conflicts. Appel had been Bruce's closest collaborator for more than three years. He served as the artist's manager, producer, and mentor, Bruce's primary source of guidance, encouragement, and protection from detractors and distractions. And Appel had gotten results, kicking open doors for Bruce, helping him grow as an artist and a performer, ushering him from being a scruffy unknown playing to half-filled bars on the Jersey Shore to being signed to a major label to performing around the nation to being declared the very future of rock 'n' roll. But having reached that threshold Bruce sensed that he needed more help to get off the doorstep and through to the other side. And in Landau he figured he'd found the perfect counterbalance to Appel.

Both men were bright, both were educated and intensely ambitious, and both were deeply musical, with feelings for rock 'n' roll that bordered on the religious. From there they went in two very different directions. Appel pursued music production in a more visceral way. He was happy to talk to Bruce about his songs, happy to do whatever he could to draw out his best, most inspired work. But he only had a certain amount of patience, particularly when they were in the recording studio, the mics were hot, and the clock was ticking. Landau, on the other hand, came at the task as an intellectual, happy to indulge Bruce's impulse to think, rethink, talk, debate, and re-rethink every move they made. "Bruce and I would get into lengthy discussions and time would pass," Landau says. "Nobody wore a watch or anything, and Mike was a dynamo. He'd come in and say, 'Okay, guys, let's go. What are we doing today? Enough of this chatter here, let's make some music!' He had the football coach thing, and had a slightly abrupt style, and a sharp tongue." Landau had a passionate connection to his vision of Bruce and his new album too, and when the two coproducers' beliefs clashed, the air between them would turn sulfuric.

The contrasting impulses and styles of the coproducers curdled the atmosphere and made progress even more difficult than it would ordinarily have been. And that was exactly what Bruce was after. It was a reflex, a pattern he'd learned as a toddler when he and his parents were sharing a house with Doug's parents, back when the young Bruce spent so much time with his grandparents he assumed they were his parents. It made sense to his young mind; Fred and Alice Springsteen lavished their time and attention on him. When Douglas and Adele got home from work they had to compete for their young son's focus. The boy, who knew nothing of the shadows that defined his grandparents' lives, understood only that the grown-ups in his home were so eager to show their love he could ask for anything. And because there was so much more at stake than any young boy could imagine he'd almost always get it, too. Once that pattern was established in his mind it became second nature for him. "It's the rule of three," Bruce told me in 2012. "My grandmother, my mom, and me. Mike, Jon, and me."

He'd do it without even realizing it. Bruce set his collaborators in opposition so he could pivot between them, incorporating what he liked about both of their approaches, even as he set them on a collision course.

If Appel had been proved correct about "Meeting Across the River," the tension between the manager/coproducer and his two coproducers had grown so fraught that Bruce began to find it difficult to focus. He was still feeling stymied by how the songs he had written leaned so heavily toward the piano, and how the overdubcentric recording style they'd adopted took him away from his customary way of working. Feeling stuck between all of his influences, Bruce decided the time had come to try something different, at least for a few days. With the Fourth of July approaching, he and Landau decided to ask Appel to take a few days off. Bruce asked Landau to break the news to their coproducer, which he did firmly but apologetically. Landau knew how he would have felt if his partners had asked him to leave the sessions, so he cushioned the blow as much as he could: get some rest, spend some time with your kids, he said. Appel's feelings were hurt, but he did as he was asked, although he also called Jimmy Iovine after a day or two to check in and see what was happening in his absence. Not very much, the engineer replied. Bruce was still spending hours staring into space feeling crushed by the pressure and saying nothing. Landau, for all his sensitivity and enthusiasm, seemed unable to reach his friend. The work stayed stalled. Finally, Bruce went back to Appel's office and asked him to come back to the sessions.

The music started to flow again, but the real disagreement lingered just beneath the surface. The bonds between Bruce and Appel weren't just personal and musical. There were also those contracts, the web of agreements Appel had drawn up for Bruce to sign at the start of their working relationship in 1972. The musician was twenty-two years old then, preoccupied with his art and completely inexperienced in the ways of business and finance. What he did know was music, and the commitment he needed from anyone he could trust to work with him. Everything Appel had said and done in the first weeks of their relationship had made his dedication extraordinarily clear, so Bruce signed all the papers without asking an attorney to explain how they would impact his life and career. And as Landau had started to surmise, that had been a mistake. Based on the sort of all-inclusive deals Elvis Presley had made with his manager, Colonel Tom Parker, the deals tied down virtually every aspect of Bruce's work as a songwriter, recording artist, and performer. The contracts had Bruce so tightly bound to Appel, in fact, that he wasn't signed directly to Columbia Records. Instead, Bruce had signed an exclusive recording deal with Appel's company, Laurel Canyon, and it was that company that had the deal with Columbia. All the deals were set to expire in 1976, and Appel was already intent on making sure his client, well on his way to completing what was beginning to feel like a breakthrough album, stayed with him. Bruce had no intention of abandoning the man who had shepherded him to this point in his career, and Landau hadn't set out to disrupt any of his friend's professional relationships. But he knew enough about the music industry to urge Bruce to at least get an experienced entertainment lawyer to look at the contracts to see what was in them.

"That was one of the hang-ups with making that album," Appel says now. "Jon kept telling him he had to get a lawyer, and all that was happening right from the get-go. And so I had all that pressure for the entire recording of that record."

This is Appel's memory speaking; nobody else remembers the talk of contracts, lawyers, and other nonmusical matters intruding in the recording sessions that summer. They had plenty of trouble just trying to get the songs on the tape sounding like they had in Bruce's imagination. But given what would happen in the wake of the caper they were trying so hard to pull off, it's easy to see why Appel might remember it that way.

John Ares / Alamy Stock Photo

Chapter 20

Tonight in Jungleland

The pursuit of "Jungleland" began near the start of the Record Plant sessions in mid-April and continued throughout the project. As the longest and most complicated of the songs, with its ambiguous characters, modular construction, and contrasting textures, "Jungleland" required greater imagination and flexibility, particularly as Bruce's sense of its sound and pace continued to evolve. Part of the challenge for Appel and Landau was in working with their artist's eagerness to try every possible option and then hold off on deciding which one he preferred. And like the city it evoked, and the artist struggling to capture its spirit, "Jungleland" bristled with sounds, feelings, and conflicts.

Much of Bruce's most melodramatic imaginings had been written in, attempted, torn out, and tossed away. The swingin' midsong digression, built on David Sancious's light-fingered piano styling, that they'd played at the Bottom Line the previous summer was a memory. The dramatic Spanish opening, all violin, castanets, piano, and snare drum reports, didn't make it out of the 914 sessions in January. By the time they got to the Main Point show in early February it had been replaced with a lyrical violin-and-piano preamble that established the darkness lurking beneath the opening. The verses themselves were set, with some minor variations on the lyrics. So the remaining riddles involved the long instrumental section that dominated the second half of the song, the Magic Rat's solitary mission through the city, his journey to the fate that awaits him in the song's closing moments. Getting this right was crucial and, so far, elusive.

They tried a variety of approaches on the instrumental piece, first giving the melody to Suki Lahav's violin, then balancing it between the fiddle and Bruce's guitar. Neither seemed to have just the right feel. They also continued to experiment with the song's conclusion, the largely instrumental piece that came after the lyric's final line. One version ended with a saxophone riff from Clemons, as if the song had wandered into a jazz club or was meandering past a street-corner musician. Another version ended with Bittan playing some spare descending chords on the piano. Still another version concluded with the same piano figure and Suki Lahav singing a high, sad melody. A fourth variation added Lahav's violin, tracing a different melody against Bittan's descending chords.

None of the possible "Jungleland" endings hit the spot. They had already started thinking of "Jungleland" as the album's final song, the last scene in what Bruce had first envisioned as the story of a day in the life of a restless young man living in a small town on the central New Jersey coast. But that version of the story faded in his imagination. The deeper he got into the record, the more he realized how high the stakes were, not just for his career at Columbia and in the music industry, but in the larger context of rock 'n' roll and in the American story.

"I was a creature who grew up in the 1950s and saw all those hot rod 1950s beat movies," Bruce says. "I thought Chuck Berry was our greatest American songwriter and I was interested in his imagery, the car and the girl. I wanted to write classic rock songs using classic rock song imagery, but I wanted to make it modern. Take the Beach Boys' 'Don't Worry Baby' and turn it into 'Racing in the Street.'"

We're back on the Jersey Shore now, 2024, on the afternoon of Bruce's seventy-fifth birthday. The summer started to fade earlier this week and he's wearing a wool cap to ward off the chill. The tequila has come out, the logs are snapping in the fireplace, and the mood has grown more reflective. All those summer memories are coming back, the sunny afternoons on the beach, the riotous noise of a bar band blasting out of the Student Prince and the Upstage. The long-ago pleasures of youth and home. And the fear that went along with it; the walls that penned you in; the voices that said you could never leave, could never make good, no matter where you tried to go. His memories of making *Born to Run* jostle with all of it. "I felt desperate, you know," he says. "That was who I was. I was that desperate character: desperate to be recognized, to be heard, to be seen. Just to transcend what I felt were the awful beginnings of my life. So I was chasing this transcendence. And my vehicle for that was the music I was writing and the shows I was performing."

Transcendence. If that's what *Born to Run* was about, and if "Jungleland" was its final word, then it needed an ending that could carry that kind of symbolic power. And when he heard the song as it was still evolving in July of 1975, Bruce knew he hadn't found it.

Bruce still couldn't figure out what to do about the Magic Rat. "Jungleland" had evolved significantly in the last year, and the fate of its central figure changed along with it. Some versions ended with the Rat and the barefoot girl reunited and walking into the dawn together. Others ended with the Rat missing, others with his death. The instrumental coda at the end of the song varied just as widely, from bittersweet jazz to rhythm & blues–like piano to violin and voice. Eventually, as Bruce focused on the darker aspects of the song, he worked with Roy Bittan to create a fuller conclusion, big modal chords Bittan arpeggiated in the style of Bach, hammering the keys as the bass notes circled and fell, a musical animation of the hero's end, balanced between tragedy and grandeur. It sounded momentous, but as a purely instrumental passage it felt remote. Was there a way to bring the listener into the heart of the Rat's experience? How could we feel what he was feeling as he met his end?

By the middle of July the sessions came down to finishing touches. Still thinking of Phil Spector and his great pop hits, they hired Charlie Calello—the arranger who had written strings for the Four Seasons, Frank Sinatra, and Neil Diamond, among many others—to compose full arrangements for "Backstreets" and "Jungleland." When he came in to conduct the sixteen-piece string section they'd commissioned, Calello was dressed in a sharply cut three-piece suit in such a vivid shade of pink Bruce began calling him the Pink Panther. Calello's arrangements were just as vibrant, particularly for "Backstreets," on which they weave in above Roy Bittan's piano during the introduction and drop in accents through the verses and throughout the choruses. By the final verse they play an octave above the other instruments, close to rivaling Bruce's vocal for prominence. Calello's strings weren't quite as overwhelming in "Jungleland," adding additional layers to the piano and violin preamble and the long instrumental passage at the center of the song, over which Clemons would perform his saxophone solo. Calello's work on both songs, Landau says, was stunning. "I thought they were fantastic."

But again, Bruce felt torn between his influences. Adding strings to "Backstreets" dampened the fury at its core; cooling its narrator's fever seemed like a mistake. The modular structure of "Jungleland" offered a wider variety of sounds and textures, particularly the instrumental sections, where the strings filigreed the core instruments with a light golden hue. If any of the string parts survived on "Backstreets," they're buried so deep in the mix they exist mostly as a feeling, rather than a sound.

While Bruce continued to work on his vocals, often rewriting lyrics as he went and adding whatever guitar parts remained to be played, the quickest overdubs came from Roy Bittan, who added his organ parts with ease. He knew exactly what Bruce was looking for and had no problem working around his own piano parts.

Progress slowed when the time came to add Clarence Clemons's solos. Bruce had figured out exactly what he wanted to hear during the breaks, and it included not just the notes and emphases, but also the intonation, particularly the bluesy falloffs at the end of some of the notes. Clemons was a uniquely emotional player, one of the rare rock saxophone players whose tone could express as much sadness and introspection as swagger. Bruce was particularly intent on hearing all of that on his new songs, and so when Clemons came in, Bruce sat with him in the studio, guiding him from note to note, pushing for this sound and that feeling, asking him to play this again, try it that way, try it again, and again, and again. The riff he played in "Tenth Avenue Freeze-Out" just after Bruce sings the line about how *the Big Man joined the band* was finished relatively quickly, but Clemons's work on the final bars of "Night" bogged down when Landau kept thinking it was out of tune. Bruce finally had to tell him he was wrong: "Jon! You're losing it, buddy!"

Bruce kept a much tighter grip on the saxophone part on "She's the One." The tune had begun as a jam, a few chords over a rhythm, and when Clemons took the lead he got just the right wail and growl out of his instrument. "He was playing the hell out of it," Bruce says now. "I wrote the rest of the song because I wanted to hear Clarence play that solo." The song developed into a standout, a hot-blooded tune set to a pounding rhythm they adapted from Bo Diddley's trademark hits. Bruce strung his vocal between pillars of awe, desire, and frustration. All of it tilted toward the climactic saxophone solo, which plays over a forty-second stretch between the end of the bridge and the song's combustible final section. At first Bruce coached him through each phrase, then had him play the whole thing.

Work on Clemons's "She's the One" solo went on and on. They ran a take, then another and another, and another after that. It went on for hours, so far past midnight that engineer Jimmy Iovine kept falling asleep in his chair. Second engineer Thom Panunzio was also visibly nodding, so Appel took the both of them out into the hallway and handed them sticks of wrapped Juicy Fruit gum. The trick was to throw away the gum and chew the aluminum foil wrapper. The sensation of aluminum on your teeth is so excruciating, he explained, there's no way to fall asleep when you're in that much pain. The younger men dutifully unwrapped the sticks, tossed the gum into the trash, popped the foil into their mouths, and bit down.

Clemons, who was already far too acquainted with the pressure cooker of Bruce Springsteen's life and career, slipped into the hot seat and leaned closer to the flames. "If you had vision you could see it. It was always just a matter of time," he told me in 2011. "All we could do was hang on. Smoke a lot of pot and just try to stay calm." Bruce, of course, wanted nothing to do with weed or any other stress reducers. He'd already found his drugs of choice. "He was getting off on the music. And on the worrying and the work."

The hands of the clock spun, the pages of the calendar fluttered past. The first half of July came and went, the deadline loomed closer. The Columbia executives wanted the record in the stores just as college students were going back to campus. For weeks Bruce had shrugged off the executives' impatience. The release date is one day, he reasoned, but the record is forever, so let's take our time and get it right. This seemed like a solid notion until Appel reminded Bruce that the record company's marketing plan wasn't the only thing dictating their schedule. They had summer tour dates booked to start on July 20, a fourteen-date run leading to a five-night stand at the Bottom Line nightclub starting on August 13. They'd canceled a stretch of shows in the spring in order to focus on recording, but with the album due and the band's accounts in desperate need of replenishing, there was no way they could back out of these dates.

And if the cash flow was important in the short run, it was even more pressing for Bruce and the band to get a running start for the Bottom Line stand in mid-August. Those would be crucial shows; Columbia had already bought hundreds of tickets and had distributed them around the building, and to key media figures in New York and the other major cities in the Northeast. At least one of the shows would be broadcast on the city's influential WNEW-FM radio station. They were already adding up to be the most important shows in Bruce's career. Given how rusty the band was after so many months off the road, they'd need at least a few weeks of steady performing to knock the dust off.

In other words: The sessions had to be finished by the morning of July 20. At which point Bruce, the band, and all their gear would have to get loaded up and hauled to Providence, Rhode Island, for the first night of the tour.

Bruce understood. He had a hard deadline; he'd conclude his work by the morning of July 20. Now that was less than a week away. But he still had to finish "Jungleland."

In Bruce's mind it had all come down to this. The last few vocals, the last guitar parts, the last saxophone solos. And then the mixing: the crucial, painstaking process of blending all the performances that go into a song, mixing them down into a finished recording. Mixing is very nonglamorous, exacting work, a collision between electronics, art, and something like spirituality. In a windowless room crowded with recording equipment and mixing consoles, the relative volume of the drums, bass, piano, organ, and guitar, and what it implies about the sound, meaning, and spiritual power of rock 'n' roll, can become not just significant but absolutely *essential*. Even if you're just talking about a four-bar span between the second verse and chorus of the second song on the second side of the album. You could fight about it for hours with the wild passion of a religious zealot. It's tricky work with just one producer and artist, but throw in three coproducers, including the artist, and two engineers, and the complexities, along with the time it takes for everyone to argue his point, multiply.

Every note and word mattered. The silence between the notes and words mattered. The length of the silence separating the songs mattered a *lot*. And nothing mattered more than every single aspect of "Jungleland." The long instrumental passage at its center had become the emotional core of what was the most intensely personal song on the album. When Clemons came in and took out his horn he knew he was in for a long and rigorous process. He knew how demanding Bruce could be. It turned out he actually had no idea. As he'd just done on "She's the One," Bruce talked Clemons through each note and passage, had him play them all individually, then together. When he had the basic form down Bruce had Clemons play the whole thing, told Iovine to roll tape, and started the recording. They got one take down, then started again. Clemons really had mastered the part, was playing his heart out, putting everything he had into the two minutes and twenty seconds of music his horn had to fill. Bruce listened, smiled and nodded, loved it. Told him to do another. *Terrific! Now do another.* It went on like that for hours.

Iovine was there for the whole thing. He has done a lot of things in the decades since he worked on *Born to Run*. Iovine has produced hit albums, started a record company, sold that company, started an audio equipment company, sold that company, worked closely with rockers, rappers, and corporate titans. But even after fifty years, the memory of what it took to record the sax solo to "Jungleland" makes his eyes widen and his mouth drop open. "Oh yeah, are you kidding me? Not only did he put Clarence through the wringer, I recorded every note of it. Right?" The process took all night, went past midnight, moved through the wee hours and into the dawn.

Did I mention that all of this was taking place on the evening, then night, of July 19, and then into the morning of the twentieth? Which is to say, the last night they had in the studio before the concert tour would begin in Rhode Island on the evening of the twentieth? This was it, there was no tomorrow for recording. The work spread across the Record Plant's studios and floors, with mixing going on in one room, the "Jungleland" saxophone solo work in another, the rest of the band rehearsing for the tour in a third. When Bruce finally walked into the rehearsal room, strapped on his Telecaster, and took his place at the center, the recording of *Born to Run* was officially finished.

Unless, of course, Bruce changed his mind. But he wouldn't do that. Would he?

A night or two earlier Bruce had told Iovine to cue up the concluding bars of "Jungleland." *I think I've got something,* he'd said, climbing out of his chair at the control panel and pushing his way through the door to the studio. He walked to the vocal booth, clapped some headphones over his ears, and stepped to the microphone. Eyes down, he nodded at the men on the far side of the control room glass and heard his voice singing the song's final lines. The Magic Rat in his subterranean warren where he lies with the barefoot girl, their hearts beating in the same rhythm. *Soul engines running through a night so tender.* They make love and then the Rat leaves to pursue his vision, whatever it is, it doesn't really matter, through the subway tunnels. Instead, he's headed off by his fate, bullets that come through the darkness and cut him down where he stands. His fate is so sudden, and so dismal, the entire city shudders. Grief floods the streets. Dreams and illusions collapse, a hard air of cruelty brings the city's poets to their knees. *And in the quick of the knife, they reach for their moment / And try to make an honest stand,* he sings in a rush. *But they wind up wounded, not even dead.* Alive but mute: a life worse than death. Bittan's piano offers a small flourish, his fingers just brushing the keys as Bruce's voice, airy, wracked by the effort that has gone into the song, into the album, into everything that led him to this point, channeled the Rat's journey to the city, through its streets, into his moment of tenderness and then his last stand in the subway tunnels. All of it leading into the lyric's final line, which he sings slowly, stretching out the gaps between the words, *Tonight . . . in . . . Jungle . . .* He holds the silence a beat longer this time, drawing it out before he finishes the word, the sentence, the story, the Rat's life: *. . . LAND.* As his voice faded in his ears, Bruce leaned into the microphone, took a deep breath, and bore down.

What happened next, Landau recalls, was a shock. Everything they'd tried to that point had flowed from the awestruck softness of the song's final lines. And what he was doing now was so intense, and so unexpected, Iovine had to lunge into the board and adjust the levels so Bruce's voice didn't shred the tape.

"That was a scary moment. Scary good," Landau says. "When it started to happen we were completely unprepared. Those *howls.*"

Is there another word that better describes the sound Bruce made next? He vocalizes wordlessly, half a dozen cries that take us back to the moment of the Magic Rat's killing: the bullets piercing his skin, the impact to his core, the explosion of light behind his eyes. And it's not just happening to the Magic Rat, because his end is also the end for Mary and the narrator of "Thunder Road," for Scooter and the Big Man, for Terry and the narrator of "Backstreets," for Wendy and the racer in "Born to Run," for the scheming gangsters in "Meeting Across the River." It's the death of dreams, of hope, of anyone who pulls out of anywhere looking to win, or just to survive. And maybe, if this last-chance power drive of an album didn't find its audience, the end of Bruce's career as a recording artist. That prospect would be painful for any artist. But for Bruce it was nothing short of existential.

For Landau—who had staked his reputation on declaring Bruce the future of rock 'n' roll, and then risked his own career as a writer, critic, and editor by signing on to be his favorite artist's coproducer—it's not a stretch to hear the songs of *Born to Run* in religious terms. "Look, the album begins with a woman named Mary," he says. And those howls at the end of "Jungleland," which is the end of the album? Landau knows what that's supposed to symbolize, too. "It ends with an allusion, in my opinion, to the crucifixion. So birth, life, and death. That's that album."

Landau knows how this sounds. He understands that he's been Bruce Springsteen's partner in music and business for fifty years. And before that he was Bruce's most prominent cheerleader. If anyone on the planet could be said to be a committed Bruce Springsteen fan it's Landau. So he's questioned his own interpretation, too. "Was it planned that way, or [am I] just some overly literary type, you know, interpreting? Well, I'm not sure exactly what I think, but I believe all those crosscurrents are embedded in the fabric of the album. And when you're talking about religion, you're talking about elevation and elation on one hand, and you're talking about pain and suffering on the other hand. And those things are all on our album."

Chapter 21

Kutztown

When it was all over—the recording, the agonizing, the mixing, the staring into space, the overdubbing, the endless nights, the lightless days—a handful of the reigning CBS executives wanted to come in and give *Born to Run* a listen. Bruce Lundvall, now the president of Columbia Records, came to the Record Plant with his new boss, Walter Yetnikoff, the former head of CBS International, now the president of all of CBS's record companies. Lundvall had been in on the project since he heard the finished "Born to Run" single a year earlier and had heard the rough tracks Landau previewed in late June, but Yetnikoff was still unfamiliar with the new songs. Now that he was in charge of CBS's entire music operation, his enthusiasm would be a key factor in how the company did or didn't support Bruce and the album.

Landau set up the listening session and prepared to play host. Bruce was happily out of town playing shows, and Appel was with him on the road, so when the appointed time arrived Landau greeted the executives and showed them into the control room. Engineer Thom Panunzio was already there, waiting at the control desk with the final mix cued up. There were a few minutes of chat, Landau unleashed some measured hype on the glories of the album, and then Landau gave the nod and Panunzio hit play.

They were hearing it for the first time, finished and sequenced. "Thunder Road," "Tenth Avenue Freeze-Out," "Night," "Backstreets," "Born to Run," and on into "She's the One" and "Meeting Across the River," then the astonishment of "Jungleland." The executives listened silently, heads nodding from time to time, a foot wagging to the beat. The Magic Rat came rolling into Harlem, launched his adventure with the barefoot girl, and then met his end. When the last notes faded the control room filled with silence. The executives sat for a long moment, eyes focused on the middle distance. Finally Landau got out of his chair, stood to face them. The silence had gotten to him; he looked nervous.

"So. Guys. Whaddaya think?"

They looked up; their eyes met Landau's. Finally, Yetnikoff spoke. He was a big man, bearded, stocky, and pugnacious, a top graduate in his class at Columbia Law School who'd never lost the rough-hewn texture of his youth in working-class Brooklyn. Yetnikoff was a visceral guy, to say the least. So what did he think of *Born to Run*?

"It's like fucking."

Bruce and the band arrived in Providence in time for the tour opener at the Palace Concert Theatre, summoned the energy to perform, and then got a day off to rest. From there they made the five-hour drive to Geneva, New York, for a one-nighter at the Geneva Theater, then turned back for an outdoor show at the Music Inn in Stockbridge (or perhaps Lenox, depending on how you read the map), a vacation spot in the Berkshire mountains of Western Massachusetts. The festival-style concert, in front of a sellout crowd of 7,000, started at 5 p.m., with the summer sun still high in the sky. The venue had a low stage, maybe four feet above the crowd, and was remarkably plain, with only the instruments, microphones, and amplifiers and little more than the barest possible lighting to highlight the performers. The band, now including Steve Van Zandt on guitar, came out in their stage wear, which looked a little out of place amid the daylit Berkshires greenery. Bruce, for his part, dressed in tight jeans, Converse sneakers, a multicolored panel shirt, a leather jacket, and a newsboy hat pulled low over his dark curls. He counted off "Spirit in the Night" to open the show, and with Van Zandt covering the guitar duties, Bruce focused on performing as a singer, slashing at the air with a hand to emphasize a lyric, doing a high kick to mark a resounding downbeat, then performing a full 360-degree spin, combined with another high kick, to end another chorus. He kept up his new style of guitar-free performing for "Tenth Avenue Freeze-Out," then hoisted his Telecaster, finally, for "Growin' Up." After taking the guitar break on that tune, he played an even longer solo on the slow arrangement of "The E Street Shuffle," trading riffs with Clarence Clemons just like the old days in the clubs. Not that the months off the road didn't leave their mark. When Bruce got to the line in "The E Street Shuffle" about the man-child giving the girls a double shot, Max Weinberg forgot to slap his snare drum twice, a lapse that caused Bruce to spin around and shoot him a quizzical smile.

Bruce was a little rusty, too. He screwed up his own part on the next song, "She's the One," when he accidentally started singing the discarded second verse and realized his mistake about half a line in, after which there was no going back. Then, just as Bruce got back on track with the lyrics, he snapped a guitar string. When the song ended he had to restring his instrument himself onstage. To fill the dead air the band reverted to another nightclub-honed strategy, turning the stage over to Clarence Clemons for an off-the-cuff performance of his old spotlight number, "Gimme That Wine." Knots of audience members leaped to their feet at the opening notes of "Born to Run," and both that song and "Thunder Road" came off without a hitch. But then Bruce vanished from the stage for an unknown reason (bathroom break?) and the band broke into "Funk Song," another nightclub-honed instrumental that featured bassist Garry Tallent. Bruce returned in time to take a guitar solo, and when it was over he leaned into his microphone. "Remember to leave the bartenders a little tip if you can!" he said, cracking himself up.

With the *Born to Run* sessions finally behind him, Bruce was clearly delighted to be back onstage. All the light-footed dancing and laughing gave him the look of a man who had finally shaken off the terrible burden he'd been carrying for nearly two years. The new songs, which they worked into the set gradually, were coming off well, particularly in cities whose radio stations had been playing the leaked tape of "Born to Run." Take all that, throw in the positive response Landau had heard directly from CBS Records president Yetnikoff, and Bruce had every reason to be happy. And so he was, for days on end, until Jimmy Iovine showed up with an acetate copy of the *Born to Run* master.

Bruce, the band, and their entourage had moved on to Kutztown, Pennsylvania, for a pair of shows at Kutztown State College, so the engineer took the train from New York. What happened when he arrived was entirely detached from reality as perceived by everyone who wasn't Bruce Springsteen. So maybe it's not surprising that their accounts are as contradictory as the things Bruce said and did when he heard the finished version of the album he had struggled so hard to create.

Maybe this is where we should think about where art comes from. The mysterious *whatever* that gives certain people the power to transform the ordinary thrum of existence—the ticking of a clock, the silent drift of clouds, half-heard voices wafting in the breeze—into the outlines of something beautiful enough to describe human possibility. Which may be biting off a lot when we're talking about something as base as rock 'n' roll songs. According to some people's estimation. But then again, art is expression, and music is expression, and rock 'n' roll is music, and also poetry, when it's done right. And if a song connects with people who experience it deeply enough for it to take root in their own imaginations, that's obviously a work of art. And not just that, but art that exists on the highest level. Which we often describe as a product of genius. And this brings us to Malcolm Gladwell.

That fuckin' guy. The author of *The Tipping Point, Blink,* and, I don't know, maybe a hundred other megaselling works of nonfiction, all of them purporting to describe and decode some complicated set of facts or events into simple equations that the reader can apply to their life. Anyway, one of Gladwell's most talked-about theories, featured in his immensely bestselling book *Outliers,* came to be called the 10,000-Hour Rule, or the "magic number of greatness," in his words, which basically asserted that anyone who spends ten thousand hours working at any one thing will be able to achieve greatness at it. So take four random young Liverpudlians, hand them musical instruments, and send them off to play nightclubs in Liverpool and Hamburg for ten thousand hours, and: meet the Beatles.

The 10,000-Hour Rule was floating in the zeitgeist when I talked to Pam Springsteen about her big brother in 2011. When her family moved away to California in 1969 Pam was still a gradeschooler, but she spent her earliest years sharing a house with Bruce. She grew up hearing him practicing his guitar in his bedroom for thousands of hours and heard about the band practices that took thousands of more hours, and then the even more thousands of hours he spent writing songs, and recording them, and on and on and on. And so, I asked her, did that put in her mind of our friend Gladwell and his rule of ten thou—

"Oh, God, no," she said. Because, she explained, Gladwell's immensely reductive theory failed to take one thing into account. The one thing that, to her mind, was the most important factor in the cultivation of genius, or greatness, or whatever you want to call it.

"It's not the ten thousand hours you spend practicing something," she said. "It's why you *need* to spend ten thousand hours practicing something."

The specifics change from person to person. They're usually different, but almost always rooted in the same thing: pain. Some kind of emptiness crying out to be filled; a desperation to transform the interior dark energy into something like light, either by the act of creation or by the adoration that comes from having created something people love. There are no universalities in the arts, certainly not among artists, so it seems safe to say that no reductive theory is ever going to describe how and why some people can create extraordinary art. But if you want to get close to the raw stuff of artistry? Look to the darkness at the core of the artist.

You didn't see it onstage, and maybe he mostly kept it bottled up when he was riding on the bus with everyone else. But somewhere beneath the leather jacket and newsboy cap, a gloom was settling over Bruce. It slipped in between the cracks of the day and filled the silence when the music ended and the cheering stopped. Did it seem like a surprising time to be gripped in the jaws of an identity crisis? After all, he'd pushed through the resistance and made his album. What's more, he'd done it in exactly the way he set out to do it, working with his own band in the studio of his choice with the producers he wanted to work with. He'd dug deep to write and then perfect the songs, and they told a story of life that felt real and true; music that *mattered*. Except what if it didn't?

And then the door flew open and the wolf came slinking in. Maybe the songs weren't as good as he thought they were. Maybe he shouldn't have let Landau talk him into all that overdubbing. Maybe it should all be harder, more raw, less slick and perfect. Maybe he'd gotten everything exactly the way he wanted it to be, but it was still wrong. Maybe he really was just a bar-band guy who should stick to dives around the Jersey Shore. Lying alone in a hotel room in those empty hours, with nothing to do but imagine all the worst possible things . . . well, he had a lot to work with. And when the final mix of *Born to Run* arrived Bruce cast his sleepless eyes upon it. And what he saw was very dark indeed.

What happened in Kutztown was so unexpected, and unpleasant, everyone seems to remember it differently. I've spoken about it to at least ten people who were there, including Bruce, half the E Street Band, Mike and Stephen Appel, Jimmy Iovine, and Landau (who was in California but was alerted by Mike Appel and then reached Bruce on the telephone), and no version of events holds from one voice to another. From what I've been able to put together, the following is either true or close enough to capture the spirit of the moment.

First, Mike Appel showed up with tape of the album's final mix. Someone had a reel-to-reel machine, so Bruce, Appel, and the band members all gathered to give it a listen. Everyone found a seat or a place on the floor, Appel hit the play button, and the music began. They all listened in silence until partway through "Jungleland," when Bruce started analyzing what he was hearing. *Oh, well, if I'm going to sing something I guess I should oversing it, that's great. Oh, and here comes the saxophone, that's* gotta *be a Bruce Springsteen record, doesn't it, nothing clichéd about* that.

He went on like that for a while, lashing out at everyone in sight, until he finally shook his head. "I dunno, man, maybe we should just scrap it. Toss this shit and start over."

That was the point when Clemons had heard enough. He climbed to his full height, turned to the door, and walked out. The others followed him, one by one, leaving Mike Appel to deal with his inexplicably inconsolable client, while Stephen Appel looked on in confusion.

Iovine rolled in not long after that, carrying special cargo: an acetate copy of *Born to Run* made from the master that would stamp the album onto vinyl and imprint it on recording tape. The mastering process can result in slight adjustments in the sound, so the engineer took Bruce off to find a stereo store that would allow them to spin the record on one of their demonstration units. They landed in a friendly establishment and pulled up some chairs to give it a close listen. Iovine cued up the disc, dropped the needle, and let 'er rip. Forty minutes later they were back on the street, Bruce in the lead, acetate under his arm as he stormed back to the hotel. The contrast in their faces would have been striking: the bearded guy moving like a tornado, wild and destructive, tailed by the baby-faced man in his wake, eyes wide, mouth slack with surprise. The hotel was built around a swimming pool, a real plus in the warmer weather, or for someone who is so disgusted with what he's carrying that the only reasonable thing to do is to take it to the poolside and fucking hurl it into the deep end.

Splash.

Then Bruce stalked into his room, threw open the door, and slammed it shut behind him. Iovine, still standing on the pool deck, watched him go, then looked to see the acetate, now lying beneath ten feet of chlorinated water. Thinking back on it now, Bruce isn't quite certain what the problem was. "I just didn't like it, you know," he says. "It was making me, you know, it just made me itchy on the inside and out." He shrugs. He's gone through a lot of psychotherapy since then, decades of work, digging through the muck of his psyche, down to the real primal stuff, running his fingers through the ooze at the bottom of the well. He can trace the darkness to his earliest days and then go back even farther, before he even existed, when the stage was being set by other hands. The hands that pulled him from the womb, the faces that looked down upon him when he arrived. The adoration, the expectation, the ghost that hovered in the air above him.

Meanwhile poor Jimmy Iovine was standing next to the hotel pool in Kutztown, his already-jumpy nervous system some combination of shocked, stunned, horrified. Was it his fault? He had no idea what had already transpired with the reel-to-reel listening session, so when he limped to the station and caught the next train back to New York he could only think of what he'd done wrong, how he should have never let Bruce listen to it on some stereo store floor model. Was it a decent stereo? Was it set up right? "You just don't know!" he says. "You don't know if the needle's right, you don't know if the speakers are out of phase. Then he took it and threw it in the pool and I freaked out." Fortunately, Iovine had come with a friend, and his friend had some Valium, so he popped one and tried to calm down.

In the hotel Mike Appel placed an emergency call to Jon Landau, who was attending a *Rolling Stone* writers conference in California. *You gotta talk to Bruce,* Appel said in a rush. *He's acting crazy, he wants to dump the whole thing, start over . . . we gotta figure this out.* Back with Bruce in his room Appel listened to his client as he paced and groused, ripping into the production, the mix, the stilted playing, his own terrible oversinging, the whole fucking disaster. Appel nodded, agreed with it all. *Yep, yep, I know what you mean, yep, I hear you.* Bruce already had an idea: it all sounded better when they played it live, anyway, so they should rerecord the songs onstage. Get a remote truck to the Bottom Line shows, record live versions of the new songs, choose the best performances, and put those out as the album. Wouldn't that be better?

Appel nodded. *Oh yeah, yeah, great idea, Bruce. I'll just call Columbia and let 'em know. They won't be happy, they may sue us, I don't know, but if you don't like the record, then fuck it, fuck the record. We'll do whatever we want . . .*

The phone rang; Landau was dialing in from California. Appel left Bruce to talk it over with their other coproducer, and the two of them got into what Landau recalls as "a somewhat combative conversation." Landau, trying to introduce something like common sense into the discussion, balanced his position between reassurance and reason. No, trashing the record wasn't a great idea, he said. He'd been there too, every step of the way. He knew what Bruce had set out to do, walked with him while he worked to achieve it, saw all the labor that went into making it happen, and now they had it. Had exactly what Bruce had set out to create, and trust me on this, he said, you got it right. It's fantastic. And if it didn't sound that way to Bruce, was he really surprised? "Do you think Chuck Berry likes to listen to his own records?" he asked. Seeing into his friend's deepest anxiety, he addressed it full-on: "You can't and will not be able to put every thought, every idea, and every creative impulse onto one record," he said. "My feeling is it's a great record, we accomplished great things, and any ideas you have from this point on, they go on the next record." With this, he knew, he'd touched the core of Bruce's deepest fear: that this record would be it, his final album, the last will and testament of his artistic life.

Landau, completing his argument: "And there's going to be a next record, believe me."

Bruce might have heard that.

Where it finally ended was in the car, on the way back to New York. Mike Appel was driving, Stephen Appel was there, Bruce, his girlfriend. Bruce was still going on and on, talking about trashing the album, starting over again, and Appel was nodding and scheming with him. If Landau had played the tough guy in the good cop / bad cop equation, Appel was being something more than the good cop. He was the crazy cop, the hell-yeah-let's-go-knock-over-the-bank-together cop. "I was being crazier than him, see," he explains. "Now he had to be the voice of reason. When he saw me getting ready to out-crazy him, he had to back down."

When Appel finished his end of the rap there was, finally, a moment of silence. Outside the scenery flashed by; they were getting closer to the city. Closer to reality. Bruce thought for a few moments longer, then shrugged. Let loose one of his dry little laughs.

"Then again," he said, "let's just let it ride."

It was July 27, 1975. *Born to Run* would be released in twenty-nine days.

Gijsbert Hanekroot / Alamy Stock Photo

Chapter 22

The Bottom Line

August 13, 1975. A rainy summer evening in New York City. The Bottom Line, a nightclub east of Sixth Avenue in Greenwich Village, was relatively small, but its four-hundred-seat capacity magnified the impact of showcase appearances for artists who could, or would soon, play far bigger halls. Bruce existed somewhere in the middle of that calculus. In some cities he had enough fans to fill large theaters and university sports centers. But there were entire regions he'd never visited, where his music had yet to ripple anyone's airwaves, where his name was entirely unknown. The best way to change that—according to his manager, his small handful of supportive executives at Columbia Records, and his scattering of fans—was for more people to see him perform.

When Bruce Springsteen had a guitar in his hand, a band at his back, and an audience at his feet, something came over him. And if you happened to see it, to hear it, to feel it, it was like walking into a dream you once had about rock 'n' roll.

It first happened in the wee hours of February 23, 1969, in a crowded all-night, all-ages nightclub on Cookman Avenue in downtown Asbury Park. He came up the stairs, trooping past the psychedelic paintings on the wall, the WELCOME TO UPSTAGE sign painted at the top, with a guitar case in one hand and a determined set to his jaw.

You wouldn't have noticed him. Bruce looked like most of the club's clientele, nineteen years old and skinny as a whisper, hair falling to his shoulders, faded jeans secured with a rope belt, on which hung the little leather pouch that held his keys, a spare guitar pick or two, and whatever money he had. Bruce still lived with his parents about twenty miles west of Asbury in the working-class village of Freehold. But he'd been hearing about the Upstage for a few months and had come in to take a look earlier in February. What he'd discovered, and returned to explore, was an overpowering sense that this was where he belonged.

He needed to belong somewhere. His father was falling apart; it was clear that his parents had to escape their hometown and take his baby sister with them. Douglas Springsteen had spent his entire life in Freehold, Adele had moved there as a teenager. The local economy had been stalled since the Karagheusian Rug Mill left town, so Bruce knew why they needed to get away and find a new start. Understanding why it was happening didn't make it easier for Bruce to absorb the loss of his home.

So here he was, guitar in hand, heading up the stairs to where Margaret Potter sat, clipboard in hand, checking in the newcomers. It was close to 3 a.m., deep in the free-form part of the Upstage's night, when the club's drums, mics, keyboards, amps, and PA system were available to any musician who signed up to jam. She noticed the new kid coming up and saw something sweet in his face as he asked, so quietly she nearly missed it, if he could play his guitar there tonight. She gestured to the front, said that's why those amps were up there, and didn't even bother writing his name on the list. Bruce smiled, said thanks, and found his way to the stage.

"I'm not sure what I was doing," he said a few years ago. "Just looking around, I guess." Or maybe he knew exactly what he was doing. "I came to stun, you know."

Six and a half years later, Bruce went to the Bottom Line with the same mission. He had his band with him and a new album full of powerful songs that might establish him on a level he could only have dreamed of a few months earlier. He'd played the same club the previous summer—a three-night stand, two shows each night, which had been successful with the crowd and with the few critics who had written about what they'd seen. But that 1974 engagement had nearly no impact on Columbia Records and the executives who, at that point, still figured Bruce for a failed singer-songwriter project from the company's Clive Davis era.

He had worked his way off the A & R department's drop list since then. But truth be told, the company's executive floors were still full of skeptics. Jon Landau's "rock and roll future" column hadn't changed many minds at the company, and neither had the buzz caused by the leaked "Born to Run" tapes. The executive previews of the *Born to Run* album earned the enthusiasm of Walter Yetnikoff and Bruce Lundvall, but that still didn't mean the company was prepared to put everything it had behind an artist whose first two albums had sold fewer than 50,000 copies between them. They figured *Born to Run* for a moderate seller that might break through in the parts of the country Bruce had worked but wasn't likely to do much business elsewhere. Thinking conservatively, they ordered 100,000 copies from the pressing plant and left it at that. Bruce, and his record, were going to have to prove they could sell more units before the company invested in making them.

But Bruce still had a small knot of supporters embedded in the company. And with the new album coming at the end of August, the Bottom Line shows took on extra significance. Columbia handed out tickets to every disc jockey, program director, newspaper and magazine editor, music writer, and critic in a position to raise the profile of their artist and the new album his advocates hoped would alter the course of his career. Assuming they could get people to listen to it. What seemed clear was that the road to the rest of Bruce's career was going to start at the Bottom Line in mid-August. And the direction it led would depend on how the shows went.

This had happened before, in another time, another place, under different circumstances. That first night at the Upstage in 1969 felt just as pressing, the stakes just as high. He'd climbed the Upstage stairs to approach a stage that served as the same crossroads. If anyone was paying attention to him in that moment it was with a flickering curiosity. He was a stranger to most of the people in the Asbury Park scene, a kid who played guitar in a high school cover band that had clomped their Beatle boots around the Monmouth County teen clubs and school sock hops of the mid-1960s. The world had changed dramatically since Bruce was in high school; rock music had opened up, become wilder and freer. The Castiles were ancient history by the start of 1969 and maybe Bruce was, too. Or maybe not. He took out his new Gibson Les Paul and plugged in. He snapped on the amplifier, heard the electric buzz swell, and took a breath.

He played a few notes, then uncorked a long, soaring run. Heads began to turn. He lowered his head, closed his eyes, and fired off another melodic blast, a spiky arc that dulled the chatter in the room, then silenced it. It was happening right here, right now. Bruce wasn't even looking at the neck of his guitar; his eyes were closed, mouth slightly open, hair hanging over his face. Deep inside himself, dwarfed by the sound he was making. It was magnetic. People stepped toward the stage, pushed in together. Suddenly the only thing anyone could see, hear, or think about was the long-haired kid wailing away on his gold-top Les Paul.

The Bottom Line shows in August 1975 sold out quickly, which they probably would have done without Columbia's massive ticket buy. But the limited quantity of tickets only increased the sense of anticipation in the city's media circles. Bruce tried to keep the shows in perspective as just another gig, but everyone knew the stakes were so much higher.

The night of the sold-out opening show, only a handful of standing-room tickets were available from the box office—the people waiting in the rain were hoping to score one of those—and with the room packed with journalists, critics, media figures, celebrity guests, and executives from every level of the CBS/Columbia corporate tower, the pressure was on.

"The whole world came to those, and not in a supportive way, either," Steve Van Zandt recalls. "It was more like a . . . 'Okay, show me something!' attitude."

He wasn't always good. Or maybe he wasn't always in the mood to try. When Clive Davis tapped Bruce and the band to join the top CBS/Columbia artists performing at the Week to Remember series of shows he booked for the Ahmanson Theatre in Los Angeles in May 1973, the executive was surprised when the dynamic performer he'd known came out looking stiff, even sullen. Davis assumed Bruce felt out of his element since he'd been playing in clubs almost exclusively and encouraged him to learn how to use the stage. "You're just standing there," Davis told his artist. "You might want to consider taking advantage of the vastness of the stage. Try moving around!" Bruce listened and nodded, but the size of the stage wasn't the problem.

Peter Philbin saw it happen when Bruce was sharing the bill with Bob Marley and the Wailers (all of whom were then billed, simply, as just the Wailers) at Max's Kansas City in the summer of 1973. Philbin had been so floored by Bruce's performance at the Troubadour in Los Angeles that winter he'd upped sticks and moved to New York so he could be closer to the action. Then he found a job at Columbia Records and made himself an in-house supporter at the label. But when he brought a bunch of colleagues to be indoctrinated during the Max's Kansas City run, he found the musician in a sour mood. "And then Bruce decides to try to play slide guitar with the microphone stand [as a slide], and it was awful. And he cleared the room." It was a rough summer for Bruce: he'd just infuriated his record company by bailing out of opening the national tour for Chicago, then Columbia's top-selling artist.

Just a few days after the Max's Kansas City show Philbin saw Bruce and the band perform at CBS's sales convention in San Francisco, and this was even worse than the Max's show.

What could Bruce have been thinking? His handful of supporters at the company were at the convention and had been mounting a whisper campaign to get the rest of their colleagues to pay close attention to Bruce's set. "So it's like me, Michael Pillot, and Peter Philbin, and we're telling the whole company, like, 'Okay, if you think he's overhyped, this will be great. Just watch the show and you'll get it.'" Paul Rappaport was one of Bruce's chief supporters at the label; he'd told everyone who would listen about the great new artist who could turn any concert hall into an evangelical church. Oh boy, were they in for something when he showed up in San Francisco! But first they'd have to sit through a few other acts. Bruce and his band were only one of the acts performing that evening and were slotted into the bill just after Edgar Winter's band White Trash, who thrilled the record company's sales force with a mini-show packed with lasers and smoke bombs. Watching from the wings, Bruce grew increasingly cross. What was he doing on the same bill as Edgar Winter? And now he had to perform on a stage still wreathed in smoke, to a ballroom full of dollar-happy executives whose corneas were still dazzled by fucking *lasers*? Fine. Fuck. Whatever.

When his turn finally arrived, Bruce opened his set with the then-unreleased "4th of July, Asbury Park (Sandy)," then stretched out his set to more than twice its scheduled twenty minutes, concluding with an extra-long version of the mini-epic "Thundercrack," including an extended guitar solo. "So then all these guys are coming up to me going, 'What the fuck was that?'" Rappaport recalls. "And I'm like, 'I don't know!'"

With the Bottom Line stand scheduled for two shows a night, Bruce would have less than two hours for each performance. That was significantly less time than he usually played, but he knew how to make it work. He engineered compact set lists that wove the *Born to Run* songs together with the highlights of his first two albums, along with covers of favorite oldies that described his roots and influences in terms of classic soul, Brill Building pop, and old school rock 'n' roll. This was the stuff of Saturday night at the Student Prince in Asbury Park—but to hear *Born to Run*, and to understand how much Bruce invested in those songs, was to hear the old songs with new ears. And to hear them performed alongside his new songs was to reexperience the entire sweep of rock 'n' roll. And, maybe, to understand its past, and possibilities, in a vastly different way.

Now Bruce makes a point of shrugging off the shows. "Just another gig," he says. But he knew what was at stake. He was still ambivalent about his ambitions and nearly as afraid of what would happen if he achieved them as he was of failure. But he had worked hard enough and struggled long enough to stop resisting his own appetite for success.

If only because it wasn't just him anymore. Mike Appel had worked so hard and sacrificed so much, and of course the band had traveled with him every step of the way. And then there were his guys at the record company, the ones who had put their own reputations on the line to keep him on the label, to get his music on the radio, to sell his records. And now there was also Jon Landau, the eminent critic–turned–coconspirator, risking his reputation and career to call him the future of rock 'n' roll.

All of these people, working so hard for so long. This time there would be no acting out, no undermining his own ambitions for the sake of some illusion of anti-commercial righteousness.

At the Upstage, back in the winter of 1969, they only had the music. All they wanted to do was come up with some cool songs and play them in a way that people liked to hear and dance to. Maybe they could make some new friends, put together a band that would have a following, maybe even get enough bookings to keep the nine-to-five world at bay for at least a little while. That's all Bruce was after, anyway. And when Vini Lopez and Danny Federici, the drummer and keyboardist who had been playing just before Bruce came in, heard the sound he was making, they ran up from the Green Mermaid coffeehouse on the floor below the main stage area. Sonny Kenn, one of Asbury's most admired guitarists since the mid-1960s, also came upstairs and saw it happen. "I thought, 'Oh my God, he's got it!'" Kenn told me in 2010. "Somehow that skinny kid was larger than life."

Lopez saw it too. "Right there, right then. I didn't need any more convincing." Bruce was nineteen, Lopez had just turned twenty. They were working-class kids, not long out of high school; their experience of life was limited to central New Jersey and the shore. School hadn't resonated, books held little appeal, the future described by their parents' existence seemed poisonous. But the long-haired guitarist pulling another wild run out of his guitar beckoned toward a far more appealing life. They were all after the same thing, and when Lopez saw Bruce he knew he was looking at the guy who could help get him there. "Imagine your rock star, and there he was: right in front of you, when he was a kid."

At the Bottom Line, August 1975, the crowd squeezed in from West Fourth Street; the seats around the cocktail tables filled up, every available inch of standing room packed solid. The lights switched off, a voice introduced Bruce Springsteen and the E Street Band, and it began. Bruce in tight jeans and Converse sneakers, his leather biker jacket over a black sweater and sport shirt, his corduroy newsboy cap perched on his thick black curls. Behind him the band launched into the opening of "Tenth Avenue Freeze-

Out," and when the opening verse came around he grabbed the microphone off the stand and hunkered down to sing into the faces of the people in the front row. *Seem like the whole world walking pretty / And you can't find the room to move* . . . He was describing the Bottom Line stage too, since seven musicians and their gear left next to no space for Bruce to operate.

He stayed low for "Tenth Avenue," then leaped to his full height to open "Spirit in the Night," emphasizing the beat by punching the air, doing a high kick, spinning around. Even without room to move he was in constant motion, diving off the stage to sing the final verse beneath the tables, then popping up to leap back onto the stage for the last chorus. Back at center stage he strapped on a twelve-string guitar and launched into the jangling opening riff of "Then She Kissed Me," the band quickly locking in while he sang, eyes closed, his face alight with memory and feeling. Then came Ike and Tina Turner's "It's Gonna Work Out Fine," prefaced with a long, funny story about a childhood friend who had gotten married and started selling insurance, then "Growin' Up" and "It's Hard to Be a Saint in the City," ending with a long guitar duel between Bruce and Van Zandt, alternately mirroring and then outdoing one another's runs. A few songs later came the *Born to Run* songs in quantity: "She's the One," "Born to Run," "Thunder Road."

Turning the corner to the encores, Bruce came out alone and sat at the piano for a solo run through the psychic shadows of "For You," then called the band out for a careering "Kitty's Back," now expanded with a comic diversion where Bruce leaped off the stage and crept through the audience, climbing into people' laps, pausing to call out friends and family ("Uncle Gene! This is my uncle Gene back here . . . this is a dangerous corner. Steven! I see your mother over here!"), creeping back to the front just in time to trigger the big *Kitty's back in town!* climax. Then came "Rosalita," even wilder and crazier than usual, Bruce digging deep to scream that key line, *The record company, Rosie, just gave me a big advance!*, then dashing out across the tabletops, sending drinks and half-eaten burgers crashing to the floor, then back to the stage, where Clemons gave chase, the two of them sprinting in a tight circle, then facing off, lowering their heads and coming together, colliding gently, locking arms, and spinning madly.

They left the stage, only to be called back by the cheering crowd, the entire room on its feet, a solid wall of sound that only quieted when Bruce returned, sweat drenched from his knees to his dripping curls. Standing at the microphone, he feigned confusion. "What? What?" He cocked his head and pointed to himself. "You talkin' to me?" There was no way he could make himself heard after that so he turned to the band and launched into Gary US Bonds's "Quarter to Three," taking another run out over the tabletops, finding his way back to the stage in time for the next chorus. *Oh, let me tell you that I never had it so good*, he sang. *Everybody was as happy as they could be.*

"Mr. Springsteen has it all—he is a great lyricist and songwriter; he is a wonderful singer, guitarist and piano player, he has one of the best rock bands anybody has ever heard, and he is as charismatic a stage figure as rock has produced."
—John Rockwell, *The New York Times.*

"The music is truly overwhelming. It touches some particularly sensitive chord, submerged deep in the rubble of the subconscious, that's exhilarating but also disturbing, because it's rarely exposed so completely. I listen to Springsteen like I used to listen to Dylan, John Lennon, and Chuck Berry—as though a life depended on it...."
—Michael Watts, *Melody Maker*

"If there is a new trend, look to Springsteen to start it. After three encores, the crowd still hollered for more at a deafening level for half an hour. I've personally never seen—or been part of—anything like it....One of the best performers in the world....Dancing on their seats. Repeated standing ovations and several encores every night.... Four encores to those who called for more a half hour after the equipment was taken apart....At times it bordered on delirium."
—*Walrus* concert reviews

FINALLY.
THE WORLD IS READY FOR BRUCE SPRINGSTEEN.

"BORN TO RUN." PC 33795
THE NEW ALBUM.
ON COLUMBIA RECORDS
AND TAPES.

Photograph © Eric Meola

Chapter 23

Flying by the Seat of My Pants

It's hard to imagine how it felt. To have dreamed of it for so long. To have spent all those hours alone in your bedroom with the guitar, the teenage bands, the years in the bars, playing for whatever wadded-up bills the drinkers tossed into the basket by the door. The endless hours on the interstate, the empty roadhouses outside towns you'd never even heard of. The breakthrough to get signed, only to learn how it felt to be bent, folded, and packaged, set up to fail on a grander scale. To live through all that and to keep going anyway. To push on and on, not because you think you're really getting somewhere, but because pushing is all you know how to do. Until the struggle became so familiar you couldn't imagine, or trust, anything else. It worked. You worked. And just when you felt comfortable with where you were, and who you were, everything changed.

"He gave two shows Wednesday that will rank among the great rock experiences of those lucky enough to get in," John Rockwell wrote in *The New York Times*. "Mr. Springsteen has it all—he's a great lyricist and songwriter, he is a wonderful singer, guitarist and piano player, he has one of the best rock bands anybody has ever heard, and he is as charismatic a stage figure as rock has produced."

Writing in *Newsday*, Tony Kornheiser looked beyond the spectacle at the Bottom Line and into the future. "I'm not the first to tell you this. And I'm not going to be the last. Bruce Springsteen is going to be a monster. It isn't a question of talent. It's a question of time."

In the New York *Daily News* Ernest Leogrande was more measured, but not by much: "For two years Bruce Springsteen's fans have been predicting that his talent will explode him into rock stardom. From the looks of his reception at the Bottom Line this week, that day finally may have arrived."

Some critics who'd seen the Bottom Line shows were more skeptical. That had to happen; it's the basic physics of the public narrative, where every action creates a reaction, where the wave that crashes onto the beach must be matched by the current pulling the water back to the sea. And so open *The Village Voice* and there was Paul Nelson writing beneath a tart headline ("Is Springsteen Worth the Hype?"), noting how those ecstatic Bottom Line sets were frankly overstuffed and at times overwrought, as if the musician felt compelled to jam every thought and idea he'd ever had into two hours, with no thought to pacing and structure and . . .

"Springsteen's weaknesses stem from too much talent, not too little. When you can achieve just about anything you want onstage, it's hard not to stay there until you've rung all the bells . . . Ironically, if he weren't as good as he is—and he is close to being the best we have—no one would be concerned with such minor issues as pace and overreach." So. Not that tart after all.

If there was one note of dissent about the Bottom Line shows it had less to do with Bruce's songs and performance than with his ascent to a higher realm of power and celebrity. Unsurprisingly, that perspective came from a writer at the *Asbury Park Press*, the hometown paper whose writers and readers had known Bruce since before he was anyone. "Outside of the Bottom Line, the boys from the Casino are dancing with their shirts open, eyes glazed," Marty Packin wrote in the dark-eyed report from the first night of the shows he filed for the *Asbury Park Press*. Describing the celebrities in the house, including the model, actress, and scenester

Cherry Vanilla and New York Knick Phil Jackson, Packin wrote like the hometown friend who had been left behind. "He's known to his several thousand ex–best friends as Brucie. 'Sure, me and Brucie go way back.' . . . And so it goes, from Little Eden to the Big Apple, from the streets of Freehold and Asbury Park to Green Witch Village [sic]. Another story in the Naked City."

Born to Run was released the week after the run at the Bottom Line ended. If the New York media had overwhelmed Bruce with acclaim for the shows, the rhapsodic praise unleashed by critics in the national publications nearly did him in. The heavyweights seemed determined to outgun one another with their ecstasies. "Mr. Springsteen's gifts are so powerful and so diverse that it's difficult even to try to describe them in a short space," *The New York Times*' John Rockwell declared. In *Creem* Lester Bangs decreed that *Born to Run* "reminds us what it's like to love rock 'n' roll like you just discovered it, and then seize it and make it your own with certainty and precision." In *Rolling Stone* Greil Marcus also reached for the superlatives, describing *Born to Run* as "a magnificent album that pays off on every bet ever placed on him—a '57 Chevy running on melted down Crystals records that shuts down every claim [for him] that has been made."

The trade publications joined the chorus too. "An immaculate musical conception," declared the unsigned review in *Cashbox*. "Nobody in years has come close to Springsteen's dizzying sense of being alive for the moment." *Billboard*'s overture came in the tongues of industrial exaltation, a Spotlight thumbnail review boxed as a Top Pick. "Sounds like the third LP from the Asbury Park kid is going to be the magic one that lifts him into the national spotlight . . . The eight cuts . . . are excellent fare for FM, and AM should also be jumping on the bandwagon." A week later the journal declared "Born to Run" one of the week's top singles, a "monster song with a piledriver arrangement . . . simply one of the best rock anthems to individual freedom ever created."

Fifty years later we can only step back, shake our heads in

wonder, and reach for another fistful of showbiz clichés: A dream come true. Everything he ever wanted. A young man standing tall in the spotlight as the cheers rain down. Artistic fulfillment, personal exoneration, happily ever after.

Except he'd been here before. Seen his name draped in laurels, been tapped for glory, declared the next big thing. But it had felt wrong back then too, and quickly went even more wrong. And then he was back where he'd started, in a rented car on an endless highway spiraling through a dismal winter day with nothing but a deserted nightclub waiting at the far end of the road.

It began when *Greetings from Asbury Park, NJ* was released on January 5, 1973. Reviews, notices, and the occasional feature started appearing two weeks later. Virtually all of them compared Bruce, his songs, and his sound to Bob Dylan. It was not the first time a young singer-songwriter had been tagged that way. As Jack Lloyd pointed out in *The Philadelphia Inquirer* on January 21, the comparison had become so common as to cease meaning anything. A legion of young singer-songwriters, especially the ones with the audacity to have dark hair and acoustic guitars, had been tossed into the same bucket: Phil Ochs, Leonard Cohen, Eric Andersen, Donovan, John Prine, and Loudon Wainwright III, to name just a few. It wasn't an insult, by any stretch, maybe even the opposite. But it certainly gave writers/critics an easy-to-reach reference point. That it was also an impossible standard nobody expected or even wanted you to meet wasn't something that concerned them.

So now comes a dark-haired, lyrically inclined, acoustic-guitar-wielding, singer-songwriting twenty-three-year-old kid from Jersey? Easy call: new Dylan. That the original BD was still there, still writing and recording and at thirty-one years old not even close to old or vanished, only made the exercise that much more absurd. "Naturally all of this is an introduction to the latest candidate," *The Philadelphia Inquirer*'s Jack Lloyd wrote in his piece headlined "Will the Next Dylan Sing Out?" "One cannot dismiss the feeling that young Springsteen is quite consciously attempting to pick up where Dylan left off with *John Wesley Harding* several years ago." Lloyd was only tentatively impressed by *Greetings* ("Once you accept the fact that he is blatantly, meticulously following the style devoted to such a fine point by a guy named Zimmerman [Dylan], it is possible to settle back and enjoy the music on these terms.") The comparisons weren't always so invidious. The critic Robert Christgau—whose *Newsday* column "Good Luck to 3 Friends Who Will Need It," published the same day, also considered the work of John Prine and Danny O'Keefe—declared himself impressed by Bruce. "His songs are filled with the absurdist energy and bleeding-heart pretension that made Dylan a genius instead of a talent," he wrote. "Springsteen has potential, and I'll play his next album the day I get it."

For his part, Bruce saw the release of his first album, and the rock 'n' roll notoriety (if not quite stardom) it would bring, as something like an oncoming freight train. Sensing himself perched on the tracks, he did his best to step out of the way and keep on going until he was nowhere in sight. In a homecoming profile that ran in the *Asbury Park Press* two weeks after the first album was released, Barbara Schoeneweis found Bruce contemplating the start of his career as a major-label pop star with a mix of anticipation and dread. "You're not your own man anymore," he said of the recording contract he claimed he'd only just allowed himself to be talked into signing. "Somehow it all comes back to money. And then other days you meet some really great people and it all feels worth it and terrific."

Speaking in what Schoeneweis called his "customarily sullen manner," Bruce refused to describe the songs on his album (the songs speak for themselves, he said) and would not answer questions about his past ("He doesn't go in for a personality image," she wrote). Schoeneweis made cursory mention of the Dylan parallel but gave her sulky subject the final word when she asked what he thought had made his music capture the ears of the men who called the shots at Columbia Records. "Well, it's me," he said.

Speaking to the disc jockey Ed Sciaky on the air at WMMR in Philadelphia in late 1974, Bruce described himself as a bystander to the start of his professional career. And not an especially willing one, either. The way he told the story, he'd been sitting on his porch minding his own business one day in 1971 when a friend pulled up and invited him to come up to New York and meet a manager who might be interested in steering his career. "I said, naw, I don't want to go to New York, I don't wanna meet these guys." When the friend rolled up with the same invitation a week later Bruce only agreed to accompany him to the city because "it was a nice night and I was totally bored, so I went up in the car and I met Mike."

He was talking about one of the most significant moments in his life, his first meeting with the man who helped lift him from being the leader of a bar band on the Jersey Shore to a major label artist. But as he continued his tale Bruce made it seem as if he'd been so disinterested in pursuing his career that he'd fended off Mike Appel's offer to be his manager for nearly half a year. "I said, 'Oh, okay, I'll think about it.' Thought about it for about five months. Went out to California."

This is what you might call a fanciful version of events. For while Bruce did indeed go to California to visit his parents, it was only after Appel had sent him away to write more and better songs. When he rang Appel a few months later it took a moment for the manager to remember him. Appel had been intrigued enough by their first meeting to invite Bruce back up to try again. The songs Bruce wrote during his California sojourn did the trick, and then some. When Appel offered to take him on as a client, Bruce accepted on the spot, then was so eager to get going he snatched up the contracts Appel gave him and signed them all without much more than a cursory look.

After placing an initial pressing plant order for 100,000 copies of *Born to Run,* the Columbia executives were surprised when advance orders from record stores added up to three times that number. They had to scramble to produce enough copies to fulfill the demand. And then the reviews started to run in newspapers around the country. These writers had ears, eyes, and access to the national magazines and newspapers that had led the conversation and set its ecstatic terms.

"Nobody in years has come close to Springsteen's dizzying sense of being alive for the moment," wrote Dale Anderson in *The Buffalo Evening News*. In the *Chicago Tribune*, Lynn Van Matre concluded that Bruce was, "certainly, one of the most distinctive and exciting forces currently on the scene." In the *Detroit Free Press,* Christine Brown made her point clear in the headline: "Springsteen Arrives, Long Live the King." The *Los Angeles Times'* Robert Hilburn wished that he'd had a copy of *Born to Run* on hand when he'd finally had a chance to meet Elvis Presley so they could have bonded over Springsteen's greatness. "I wanted somehow to show him, amidst a stream of other well-wishers that evening, that we had a strong musical affinity . . . [and] now we have someone with the ambition, instincts and vision to put some of the pieces back together. That's where Bruce Springsteen comes in. He is the purest glimpse of the passion and power of rock 'n' roll in nearly a decade."

The critical raves pumped up album sales, which sent *Born to Run* skipping up the *Billboard* charts, peaking at number 3 in early October. The *Record World* charts, configured by a different calculus of sales and radio play, put *Born to Run* at number 1. The single of the title track peaked at number 23 in *Billboard*'s Hot 100, but in the mid-1970s, when albums drove the industry, the success of the full record dictated perceptions of the moment. The blizzard of reviews in turn drew more attention to the tour, which headed southeast in early September, then swung north to the upper Midwest and back east again in early October, leading to a pair of emotional homecoming shows at the Monmouth Arts Center theater in Red Bank on the eleventh.

Bruce opened the first performance with "Meeting Across the

River," the first and only time that song has launched a concert. Here in his hometown (or just a few miles north of it, close enough to feel like home), surrounded by the broken-down bars and drafty houses he'd lived among, recalling his own desperation to become something more, the willingness to risk everything for even a long shot at glory, the tale of the desperate small-timers risking it all to take one last chance felt exactly right. He sang it for his friends, neighbors, and fellow travelers. He sang it for himself. And for the two teams of reporters from New York who were already preparing to launch him so far into orbit he'd never be able to come home again.

He hated the Dylan comparisons. It was the worst kind of hype, he said. The type of fiction the media makes up about you because they can't be bothered to listen to what you do, let alone think about it long enough to hear what you're saying, let alone understand it. Bob Dylan, he said, had nearly nothing to do with what he was doing, what he was thinking. He distanced himself the best he could. "I like the cat," he told *Rolling Stone* in 1974. "The similarities are probably there somewhere. But we come from two totally different scenes, you gotta remember that." He made the same point to a reporter from *Time* who came by around the same time. "The best thing anyone can do for me is not to mention Bob Dylan," he said. "I've been influenced by everybody from Benny Goodman on. Sam Cooke, Wilson Pickett, Fats Domino. When I was nine and saw Elvis Presley on TV, I knew that was where it was at."

But he'd paid close attention to Dylan, and not just to his music. Bruce also saw how Dylan molded his past to serve his vision of his present and future, who he was and who he intended to become. How Bobby Zimmerman, son of a comfortably middle-class furniture store owner in Hibbing, Minnesota, became Bob Dylan, blowing into town on the back of a freight train. A child of the circus who took his rest in hobo camps, who modeled himself from the clay of an America so old and weird his imagined past was truer than the facts of the matter could ever be. The fictions served multiple purposes, making him mysterious and cool, putting an intriguing spin on his music, and also steering prying eyes away from tender secrets he preferred to keep to himself. So when the buzz from his shows began to resonate in mid-1974, Bruce answered questions about his past with exaggerated tales from a hard-luck childhood that he'd only just survived in one piece. Why did he leave his hometown? "It was simple, man," he told Jeff Hinkle from the South Jersey *Courier-Post*. "I couldn't walk down the streets of Freehold, NJ. It was violent—you'd get into very bad situations." In 1974 he told a group of European reporters that he'd been a habitual runaway as a teenager, perpetually ditching his parents' home to live on the streets of New York. But that version of events clashed with the equally fanciful tale he told *The New York Times*' John Rockwell a year later about how his parents had moved to California when he was still in his midteens, leaving him to finish high school and start his career without a home or parental support.

Sitting in his living room five decades later, Bruce considers his younger self's machinations through a crooked smile. "I'm sure I was, um, embellishing a little," he says. "Suddenly I'm in the midst of this big business, and I'm, you know, flying by the seat of my pants."

In the wake of Jon Landau's rock 'n' roll future column in mid-1974, Appel started making another one of his outrageous demands to writers and editors eager to write about his client. They could write whatever they wanted, he said. But the only way to secure an interview with Bruce Springsteen was to put him on the cover. It didn't matter who you were or how big and important your publication was. No cover, no interview. The requirement was outrageous for an artist of Bruce's commercial stature, and also nonnegotiable. Mostly it served to keep Bruce free of pesky reporters. And when a publication played along, the coverage enhanced his reputation in a way an ordinary article never could. Appel saw no reason to change the policy for the release of *Born to Run*, and when an editor from *Newsweek* got in touch with the manager late in the summer he had surprising news: the buzz from the Bottom Line shows had convinced the top editors that they could, and should, put Bruce on the newsweekly's cover. Writer Maureen Orth led a team of reporters to work on the piece.

When news of their project traveled a few blocks east to the offices of *Newsweek*'s primary competitors at *Time* magazine, arts writer Jay Cocks, who had been following Bruce's career since the release of *Greetings from Asbury Park*, was irate. Sources who had been interviewed by the *Newsweek* team got the sense that they were preparing a hit piece, focused less on Bruce and his music than on the industrial machinery that was attempting to turn him into a star. "I thought it would be a killing representation of an important American artist," Cocks told me. He lobbied his editor and soon *Time* was working on its own cover story. Both magazines had committed to putting Bruce on the cover. Neither wanted to be scooped by the other. He was back on the railroad tracks but this time there were two trains bearing down on him, coming from opposite directions.

Chapter 24

Backlash

When *A Hard Day's Night* came back to theaters a decade or so ago, I took my kids to see it. On the drive home, my middle son wondered how the global eruption of Beatlemania, featuring the Liverpool lads at their wisecracking, *yeah-yeah-yeah*–ing cuddliest, had impacted the band's reputation. Had the critics and serious fans accused the band of selling out? What he couldn't have known as a teenager in 2014 was that in 1964 the concept of *selling out*, in which a musician is scorned for exchanging their artistic credibility for fame and wealth, didn't exist. It took the Beatles' epochal career, the way they transformed rock 'n' roll into an engine for artistic expression and cultural commentary, to make anyone think a rock 'n' roll song could be important enough to be corruptible. By the end of the 1960s rock and soul music had become the soundtrack to the youth counterculture. Almost every song in the top ten seemed freighted with layers of political and cultural meaning. And the corporation known as Columbia Records, a subsidiary of the behemothic media empire CBS, was selling its products with advertisements declaring "THE MAN CAN'T BUST OUR MUSIC."

By 1975 the tension between art and commerce was a definitive factor in critical analyses of popular music, particularly when it came to artists who presented as substantive. Which artists were real and which were phony? How could you tell the difference between a legitimate phenomenon and a corporate hype? For Bruce, who had invested himself entirely in his music and career, it became a fundamental concern. When people wrote or talked about his work, they were describing the essence of his soul. When he wrote and recorded *Greetings from Asbury Park, NJ*, it felt like an expression of his deepest, most tender feelings. And what they said about him was: *Bruce Springsteen is the new Bob Dylan.* "They came out with the big hype," Bruce complained to *New Musical Express* a couple of years later. "I mean how can they expect people to swallow something like that?"

It had taken a year and a half to work his way out of that shadow, and then came Landau's rock-future column. "And I'm just getting over this Dylan thing—oh, thank God that seems to be fading away—and I'm thinking thank God people seem to be letting that lie and *phwoooeee*! 'I have seen . . . ' No! It can't be!" He laughed and shook his head. "It was really a nice piece and it meant a lot to me but it was like they took it all out of context and blew it up and who's gonna swallow that? Who's gonna believe that?"

Actually, Bruce Springsteen did.

Or he wanted to, in the worst way. But he also didn't believe it at all, in an even worse way than that.

That same cognitive and emotional dissonance had lived within his chest since he was small, when he divided his days between the grandparents who beheld his arrival as the return of the precious child they had lost, and the father who couldn't keep his own demons from visiting their cruelties upon his son. *The chosen one or a waste of space.* On any given day Bruce could feel like either one. Or both.

"So I was balancing both of those things all the time and trying to prove that, no, I'm the golden boy. I'm the champ." But what if they didn't believe it? And how could anyone believe a claim about a rock star that came at them from the covers of the two biggest and most powerful outlets at the center of the mainstream media?

October 20, 1975.

The magazines came out on the same day. This only made it more unbelievable. *Time* and *Newsweek* were at the height of their influence then, the point at which their power to define current events and dictate the national narrative was unrivaled. For a rock musician to be on either magazine's cover was a big deal. Fronting both in the space of a year would have been extraordinary. In the same month, all the more so. But appearing on the cover of both magazines in the same week? On the strength of your first hit album? That was uncharted terrain.

As *Time*'s Jay Cocks had surmised, the *Newsweek* story focused less on Bruce's music than on the corporate machinations surrounding the release of *Born to Run*. With a cover line reading "Making of a Rock Star," the piece, written by Maureen Orth, noted Bruce's powers as a performer and songwriter but spent more time on Columbia's publicity campaign, Mike Appel's aggressive management techniques, and a few tart dismissals from executives at competing record companies. Cocks's piece in *Time*, "Rock's New Sensation," on the other hand, focused on the music and the artist's long journey from Freehold to the threshold of mainstream success.

Viewed side by side, as many consumers first saw them on the newsstand, and then in a wave of stories analyzing how the competing stories had come to be, the dueling Springsteen covers were momentous. Whether you interpreted his ascent as a heartening story about the rise of a hardworking young artist or as a new low in the annals of corporate chicanery, another step down from The Man Can't Bust Our Music, was up to you. And depended, perhaps, on your tolerance for any rock star who dared to speak in terms of faith, hope, and redemption.

When the magazines—dated October 27—hit the newsstand, Bruce and the band were at the Sunset Marquis hotel in Los Angeles taking a few days of rest in the wake of a four-night stand at the Roxy nightclub, the West Coast equivalent of the Bottom Line shows, intimate performances for audiences heavy on industry and media figures and showbiz celebrities.

Steve Van Zandt was the first member of the band to see the magazines. He'd gone to a newsstand and come back to the hotel with an armload of *Time*s and *Newsweek*s, tossing copies to everyone he saw, shouting and laughing. Bruce was lounging by the hotel pool. When the guitarist showed up and started throwing magazines around, he leaped up from his chaise, sprinted into his room, and slammed the door.

"He was pissed!" Van Zandt says. "I was laughing, I thought it was fun. Seeing your friend on *Time* and *Newsweek* is completely surreal. I mean, just imagine. But it was certainly funny."

For Mike Appel it was an unalloyed triumph. After three years of shouting his client's praises with the brashness of a latter-day Barnum, he'd pulled off the most audacious publicity move he'd ever even heard about. At the start of his career, he'd followed the example of Elvis Presley's manager Colonel Tom Parker. But now he'd done the Colonel one better.

"And on my birthday, too!" he told me. "How's *that* for a birthday present!"

For Appel it was a gift, but Bruce felt like he'd been pushed to the lip of a great psychic chasm. Hero or loser? Legitimate artist or corporate-made phony? The voices he was so used to hearing in the back of his mind had projected themselves onto the covers of *Time* and *Newsweek,* where literally everyone in the fucking world could hear them.

Desperate for escape, he snuck out of his room to spend the rest of the day shooting pool and playing pinball with former CBS publicist Frank Shargo and Columbia publicist Ron Oberman.

That Shargo, who had taken a job at another company, was the publicist who had created the full-page ads that ran after Jon Landau published his *Real Paper* column in mid-1974 underscored the complexity of Bruce's ambitions and fears.

"Ambivalence is my lifetime condition," Bruce says now. And not just about the riddles his family had planted in his consciousness. As Stephen Appel knew, Bruce was only too aware of how deadly rock-star-caliber fame could be. "He was worried that fame was evil," Stephen says. "He'd idolized artists who killed themselves. People getting lost in their own caricatures. He knew it could ruin people's lives."

Some critics didn't get it. This is inevitable in matters of taste. Nothing can ever be unanimous, different ears hear things in different ways—the first notes of the song that make your spirit leap for joy make me cringe. The polite thing to say under these circumstances is as little as possible. No point in yucking someone else's yum, after all. Except arts criticism does not exist to be polite. And for the pop music critics of the 1970s, when different styles of rock 'n' roll music seemed to animate different social and political beliefs, the emergence of a new album or artist held implications that went far beyond music.

The first wave of skepticism about Bruce and *Born to Run* came before the *Newsweek* and *Time* covers, in response to the chorus of rave reviews issued by the nation's most elite critics. How could it be that the likes of Greil Marcus, Lester Bangs, John Rockwell, and Robert Christgau, to name just a few, could all be so very dazzled by the same album? And to what extent did their shared enthusiasm have to do with the fact that *Born to Run* coproducer Jon Landau was not just an elite critic himself but also the editor of *Rolling Stone*'s record reviews section? If you wrote for a local daily in a midsized industrial city, say, you might be tempted to dismiss their shared opinions out of hand. Consider, for instance, Mike Kalina, a music critic for the *Pittsburgh Post-*

Gazette. "[Springsteen is] the artist every rock critic seems to be raving about, for some unknown reason," he wrote, going on to note that no amount of critical praise had done much to expand Bruce's audience. "Perhaps because he is lousy." Kalina expanded upon his assertion, critiquing the artist's diction, his lyrics, and the layered production that struck his ears as "cluttered."

But the first truly substantive dissent came from England in early September via *New Musical Express*'s Roy Carr, who dismissed *Born to Run*'s creator as a purveyor of what he called "Bogus Outlaw Chic." The critics who celebrated his music, in Carr's estimation, had been taken in by "an extremely astute— though not greatly inspired—*ideas man*." Who, he implied, might not be the artist himself. "I've got to hand it to Springsteen," Carr wrote. "Or somebody." Ouch.

In the United States the first high-profile denunciation of *Born to Run* came from Henry Edwards in *The New York Times*, whose column, published on October 5 and titled "If There Hadn't Been a Bruce Springsteen, Then the Critics Would Have Made Him Up," was as much a pan of other critics (including his fellow *Times* man John Rockwell) as of Bruce and his album. Even so, Edwards had plenty to say about the many "conspicuous flaws in [Bruce's] music making," e.g., his "harsh baritone" voice, too-dense instrumentation, and riffs that struck Edwards as entirely too reminiscent of other artists' work. And though Edwards acknowledged that some aspects of the album might grow on a listener over time, he also noted that the "knowledgeable listener" would hear enough echoes of other artists and songs to understand that Bruce was more a collagist than the creator of original music. "Those not infected with rock music nostalgia may be forgiven if, after the first ten minutes of hearing Springsteen sing, they find the hoopla tiresome and the performer vacuous," Edwards concluded. Predictably, perhaps, Edwards's column was the most prominent work of criticism featured in *Newsweek*'s hype-focused cover story.

Still, it was those dueling *Time* and *Newsweek* covers that triggered the biggest wave of *Born to Run* revisionism that fall, just eight weeks after the album's release and the initial euphoric reception. The appearance of the same relatively obscure musician on the covers of the nation's two top news magazines crystallized some observers' preexisting suspicions about groupthink in the New York media. To the deeply skeptical, the mere fact of the matched set of Springsteen magazine covers was clearly evidence of the mass media's stupidity or venality. They're either idiots or all in on it together, engaging in some kind of corporate-celebrity sales-and-cash-collecting daisy chain. "Nobody has the slightest idea what they're talking about," declared the *San Francisco Chronicle*'s John L. Wasserman, pointing to a few factual inconsistencies that appeared in the two cover stories. Is it a cheap shot to point out that Wasserman follows his dig on the newsweeklies' carelessness by misidentifying Mike Appel as Bruce Appel? Or that the *Chicago Tribune* columnist Mike Royko's assertion that rock critics had written entire articles about how the musician had used the exhalation "Huh!" in the lyrics of "Born to Run" was a figment of his own imagination? Or maybe those faulted examples simply underscore how anyone who becomes the subject of that much media attention will inevitably be reduced to an abstract symbol in a completely different conversation.

It went on like that through the fall, the two varieties of backlash—against the too-slick, all-powerful major media and against the mostly unknown rocker from Nowheresville, New Jersey, aspiring to mainstream acceptance. The constant media attention kept sales humming, pushing the album to gold status in early October, from which it kept climbing. At the same time concert agent Sam McKeith had booked the band into cities and states Bruce had never visited, out west to Seattle, Portland, and Sacramento, then back east to Omaha, Oklahoma City, Kansas City, and more. They revisited cities where they'd once played near-empty nightclubs (Dallas, Miami) and cities they had worked relentlessly. McKeith set the shows into concert halls, sometimes for multiple nights. The crowd sizes could vary widely, and not always predictably (Seattle's Paramount Theatre sold out immediately, Portland's Paramount Theatre was half-empty).

"There were places where people loved us, and there were places where, because of the hype, they just panned us to the moon," Bruce says, his face alight with his memory of the days when he still had so much to prove. "Some of it was great, some of it was terrible, and I made the mistake of reading every review in every town for the entire tour. And I was still very young, so I took a lot of it to heart."

In mid-November Bruce and the band made their first journey across the ocean, flying to England to launch a four-date foreign tour set to start with a much-anticipated London debut at the Hammersmith Odeon theater. From there they'd hop to the Continent for shows in Stockholm and Amsterdam before concluding the venture in London with a second show at the Hammersmith Odeon. Unfamiliar with foreign countries and still stung by the fallout from the *Born to Run* hype-fest that had consumed the last few months, Bruce came to London feeling somewhere between wary and paranoid. He was exhausted by it all: the publicity, the criticism, the sound of his own name. All he wanted was what he had always wanted: a chance to play his music the way he felt like playing it, without getting drowned out by the endless media brouhaha. Was that too much to ask? Apparently so.

When he got to the theater, Bruce discovered the marquee glowing with the words FINALLY, LONDON IS READY FOR BRUCE SPRINGSTEEN AND THE E STREET BAND. He was set immediately on edge—even more so when he got inside and realized that each and every seat in the place had been festooned with banners and handouts with Jon Landau's "I saw rock 'n' roll future" quote. Bruce's cork popped. He stormed the hall and tore the signs off the seats, yanked the banners off the wall, shredded every piece of paper he could get his hands on, bellowing that he wasn't gonna play nowhere covered in this shit, before sprinting back to his dressing room to try to regain his composure.

Too much hype, too much talk. Just as Bruce had feared, it had drowned out the music and made him a caricature of himself. By the time he took the stage at the Hammersmith Odeon, he came with a wool hat pushed down over his eyes, as if he already knew how badly he and his band would be received. He was so convinced that the publicists' gaudy attempts at myth-building had undermined any chance he had of connecting with the London crowd, no amount of cheers or applause could convince him that they were having a good time. "We played four shows, got sandblasted, and scooted home," he told me of that first European swing. It was the opening disaster at the Hammersmith Odeon that set the dismal tone of the trip, he said.

Except that wasn't what happened. Even if the British audience strained a little to grasp songs that many of them were hearing for the first time, the interchange between artist and audience captured in the film and live recording is every bit as passionate as it was at the shows back home in the United States. The tape doesn't lie. The crowd is hushed for the quiet songs, alive with energy to match the fast ones, cheering all the while. At the end, the audience is on its feet shouting for more. Reviews of the show noted the distraction posed by the overheated publicity, and some identified lapses here and there. But the vast majority of notices were positive.

None of it changed Bruce's own estimation of the experience. Which was so sour in the aftermath of the Hammersmith Odeon show that he decided to bury the film of the show that had been shot for British TV's popular music program *The Old Grey Whistle Test*. He couldn't stand to look at the film for nearly thirty years. Maybe because he'd pushed himself past the point where he could absorb more applause. Because his feeling of being under siege didn't require an actual attack. The calls, as the saying goes, were coming from inside the house.

Chapter 25

The Other Thunder Road

Sitting in the living room of his beach house on his seventy-fifth birthday, Bruce is nursing a tequila and thinking about everywhere he's been and how he got there. The concert on the beach at Asbury Park the week before wasn't intended to summarize his career; no single three-hour show could come close to doing that. But being back where his career began put him in a celebratory mood. "Going back home!" he says.

And if he has come a long way from the scuffling kid he was when he started out in the late 1960s and early 1970s, Asbury Park has remade itself, too. Buildings that were once abandoned downtown have been reclaimed and revived. New restaurants, bars, and hotels have risen near the boardwalk. "We were there when no one was there, you know," he says. "The town fought to revitalize itself, and to finally play on the beach in Asbury Park with thirty-five thousand or forty thousand people there, it was a historical moment. And I think for the town to kind of put the cherry on top of the cake they've been making over the last few years."

So much of the music he made, so much of the artist and cultural figure he became, can be traced to *Born to Run*. The irony is how the most vivid characters on the album all have the same goal: to leave the town full of losers; to hit the road; to get to the place where they really want to go, where they'll hit it big, live in love, and walk in the sun. That's what he wanted then, too, and it's who he was on the album. *The guy who leaves,* as Steve Van Zandt says.

But by the time of *Darkness on the Edge of Town* in 1978, he had become someone else altogether: *the guy who stays.* It was a significant move, Van Zandt says, particularly for an artist coming off his first hit album. "Man, you know, you're one of the very few that you know the audience can find. They find you, and then they define you, and you're encouraging that. 'This is who I am.' And then to completely change that persona, like a hundred eighty degrees, you know. And say, 'Listen, that wasn't really who I am. *This* is going to be who I am, and it's quite different.'"

It also reveals something of the man who isn't quite joking when he says that his most consistent attitude about life, the world, and everything is: ambivalence.

Bruce was never quite who he was supposed to be. It began years before he was born, when his own father was a little boy and his big sister, Virginia, went out to play with a friend. They were on their tricycles, racing down Randolph Street in Freehold, when an oil truck came thundering around the corner. The other girl got out of the way but Virginia was struck by the immense vehicle, her body shattered by its wheels. The death devastated her parents. Fred and Alice Springsteen were so undone by the tragedy they lost their ability to care for Douglas, their remaining child, and he was sent to live with relatives. Douglas eventually came home, but Virginia's absence cast a chill through the family. Maybe the anguish had always been there. A dark thread ran through the Springsteen DNA. The family was full of relatives who either lurked in the background or made you wish they would. There would be fits of mania, then abrupt descents into gloom. Days, weeks, months spent alone, a person reduced to a red cigarette ember floating in a lightless room. Fred and Alice inhabited the darkness from the moment Virginia died until the day in late September 1949 when Douglas and his wife, Adele, came home with the first new light to enter their home since Virginia's death. His name was Bruce Frederick Springsteen.

Fred and Alice took the baby as their own and lavished adoration on him. The younger Springsteen couple, Doug and Adele, had moved in with Doug's parents when their son was born, and because they both worked full-time Fred and Alice became Bruce's primary caregivers. When he was old enough to consider who was who in his life he assumed the older couple were his parents. "It was very emotionally incestuous and a lot of parental roles got crossed," Bruce told me in 2011. All the toddler knew was that Fred and Alice saw him as a walking miracle. Their dead daughter revived in new form. Through their eyes, everything he did was perfect. Anything he wanted could be his. Adele Springsteen had a more realistic perspective about her son, and eventually told her husband they had to get their own home. Douglas's own perspective, meanwhile, was subject to internal currents he couldn't always navigate. As Bruce got older, Douglas was increasingly beset by demons. His attempt to gird his son against the world's brutality came out sounding like contempt. Adele adored her children (a daughter they named Virginia joined the family soon after Bruce's birth, and Pamela came in 1962) and gave her son the love and structure he craved—but the disjunction, the extraordinary love and icy contempt he felt within his family, defined Bruce's consciousness.

"I had the ego and empowerment of having been the golden child, right? But at the same time, I'd had my dad, who was telling me that I wasn't worth anything," Bruce says, gazing into the fireplace. "So I was constantly trying to prove that to anybody who listened, really, because I lived a long time as an underdog and on the downside of things."

In a town full of losers, say . . . But despite his desperation to get away to somewhere, anywhere, different, he could never stay away. He'd get there, look back over his shoulder, and feel the pull toward home.

What started as the opening to *Born to Run* has become one of his most beloved songs, a reliable pivot in the emotional current of a show, the point where the darker notes struck by the songs he plays in the middle of the set take a turn to the light. Look at it closely and you'll notice that "Thunder Road" has the same structure and themes as an entire Bruce Springsteen concert. It starts quietly, then pulls out of the station at a measured pace, touring the pitfalls of life. The broken love affairs, the inevitable losses, the wishes that go unanswered. But the highway beckons and when the couple resolves to leave together, the song shifts into overdrive. *I'm pulling out of here to win!* Bruce cries, the drums rain thunder, and then it's an anthem, those ringing Aaron Copland–esque chords, the blaring saxophone, Bruce on his knees, sliding across the front of the stage, a moment of unalloyed triumph. He gave up the knee slides after 2012 or so, but "Thunder Road" was a staple on his most recent tour, usually sandwiched between "Badlands" and "Born to Run." After that the party really got started: "Glory Days," "Dancing in the Dark," "Tenth Avenue Freeze-Out," "Rosalita," on and on. All of it coming on the far end of "Thunder Road."

But that's not how Bruce always saw the song. One of the curious and unexplained outtakes from *Born to Run* is an alternate version of "Thunder Road," a stark reimagining that kept the lyrics mostly intact but stripped the familiar music away, replacing it with a largely monochromatic set of chords strummed on an acoustic guitar. The melody is different too, flattened and chilled. In this iteration the narrator starts out subdued. By the time he gets to the final line, the part about the town full of losers, he sounds numb. Like a guy who's miles away from believing that he could ever get anywhere better, let alone remake himself into a winner when he gets there. Hope has simply become a habit he can't break.

The lyrics are much closer to the final version he recorded for the album than to the "Wings for Wheels" version he performed as late as February 1975, dating this version of the song to the late spring or early summer of that year. Whenever Bruce recorded it, he didn't seem to have done it at the Record Plant or anywhere that would have sent its tapes into Bruce's recorded archives, which he sold to Sony Music in 2021. When I played the song off my laptop to a room full of Sony executives during the summer of 2024, their mouths fell open. Where did you *get* this?, they asked. Actually, it's not hard to find. The acoustic "Thunder Road" has been circulating on bootlegs for at least twenty years. And like nearly everything else in the world it's available online.

Bruce's memory of this version of the song has evolved over the years. When I first asked him about it in 2011, he couldn't recall the specifics, but it definitely rang a bell. "It must have just been something I wanted to try, you know," he said. "We did a lot of experimenting on that record, and I'm always second-guessing myself so it must have been something I took a swing at."

Was it true, as someone had told me, that he'd considered starting the album with the optimistic, full-band "Thunder Road" and ending it with the gloomier solo version? Bruce thought it over for a moment. "I don't remember that, but it sounds like the kind of thing we might have talked about," he said.

When I brought it up again in the fall of 2024 he said he had no idea what I was talking about. "We had 'Jungleland' at the end, and that was really the final word." True enough. But so is the fact that the place the Magic Rat ends up in "Jungleland," gunned down by his own dream, is exactly where the highway in the alternate "Thunder Road" was leading.

Born to Run sold 700,000 copies by the end of 1975 and moved past the one million mark early in 1976. That achievement was overshadowed by the growing conflict with Mike Appel over those contracts Bruce had signed in 1972. Had he read them, or handed them to a lawyer, Bruce would have understood that the deals encompassed every aspect of his work, management, record production, and song publishing, and granted Appel an outsized amount of the income and authority over where, how, and with whom Bruce recorded. What had been standard in the days of Elvis and Colonel Tom Parker now seemed usurious and wrong, and when they couldn't negotiate a new way forward—Appel offered to revise the deals in Bruce's favor if he extended the management deal, Bruce offered to continue on a handshake deal that either could exit if and when they wished—the conflict blew into a pitched legal battle. The conflict kept Bruce out of the recording studio for nearly two years, tied up all the money he should have earned from his hit album, and nearly capsized his career just as it was taking off.

Bruce could handle the financial strain of litigation; he was used to being poor and having to struggle from gig to gig. But losing control of his music was intolerable. And falling out with the man whom he'd come to depend on in so many ways was the worst. Appel was a good man whose dedication to and sacrifice for his client's music matched Bruce's own level of commitment; he'd become not just a partner but a father figure. Appel's initial impulse was to accept Bruce's offer of a handshake deal, but his own father, a tough customer who ran a successful real estate business, urged his son to stick to his guns and the deal came apart. All the gory details of the litigation, and the opposing parties' arguments over the constituent points, are available elsewhere. But the grief Bruce felt over the rupture can be heard most clearly in "The Promise," a song that emerged in the midst of the struggle and that was eventually released, first as a newly recorded bonus track on his 1998 box set *Tracks*, then in a vintage full-band version unearthed to be the title track to the two-CD set of *Darkness on the Edge of Town* outtakes released in 2010.

To be clear, Bruce has repeatedly denied that "The Promise"

has anything to do with Appel or their legal battle. "I don't write no songs about lawsuits," he said back then. And of course he doesn't, in any literal sense: what, after all, rhymes with *interrogatory*? Instead, he told the story of a racer who built his car with his own hands, picked up a few wins, took on an investor to keep going, won the big race, and went west to live the dream that comes after a big racing triumph. *But somehow I paid the big cost*, Bruce sings. *Inside I felt I was carryin' the broken spirits / Of all the other ones who lost.* In the end he's broke and alone by the side of the road, preparing to sleep in the back of a car that doesn't even belong to him.

For a song that isn't about a lawsuit, "The Promise" is very much about how it *feels* to be embroiled in a lawsuit. Particularly one that sets you against a man you love, who loves you and helped make you who you are but can no longer serve as the father figure he once was. The pain in the song is almost unbearable and would be hard to listen to if Bruce's real story had ended differently.

> *Thunder Road, for the lost lovers and all the fixed games*
> *Thunder Road, for the tires rushing by in the rain*
> *Thunder Road, remember Billy, what we'd always say*
> *Thunder Road, we were gonna take it all and throw it all away*

Here's another unresolved story from the *Born to Run* era that gives us another glimpse at that stubborn ambivalence. This one takes place at the Bottom Line, after one of the epic performances that launched the album, and Bruce, into the stratosphere. Stephen Appel, Mike's brother and Bruce's road manager in those days, was with him in his dressing room, handing the sweaty musician his towels and water, and paused for a moment to ask about one of the new songs he'd just performed. Specifically, he wanted to know about that line near the end of "Jungleland," just after the death of the Magic Rat, that describes the silence of the witnesses. "That part where he says, *The poets down here / Don't write nothing at all, they just stand back and let it all be,"* Stephen said. "I told him I didn't get that line. He was sitting there sweating, his head was down, and then he looked up and said, 'That's because I'm the poet.' And that's all he said. He never said another word about it. And it was kind of scary when he said it. I was thrown off by it."

Bruce, with a dismissive shrug: "That doesn't sound right. In those days I'm twenty-four years old, I'm really not that analytical, and I'm certainly not that self-analytical as of yet. I'm really just writing things and I'm coming up with a line that feels good to me. Those lyrics were just instinctively written."

So did Stephen just dream the whole encounter? It seems like a strange thing for him to have made up, especially given how many of his other recollections are confirmed by Bruce and others who were there at the time. But sometimes memory takes on a life of its own. Bruce has no memory of the acoustic "Thunder Road" either, and you can hear that on YouTube.

What Bruce doesn't remember often seems to come down to his sense of faith and what constitutes a miracle. Of being the golden boy who makes miracles happen simply because he *is* magic, as opposed to the striving professional who actually has to work at it. The Great and Powerful Oz, not the little man pulling levers behind the curtain.

Bruce and Appel reached a settlement in the spring of 1977 and Bruce rushed back into the recording studio, this time with Jon Landau as his sole coproducer, to start making his follow-up to *Born to Run. Darkness on the Edge of Town* was released to even more critical acclaim and solid sales a year later. An arduous yearlong concert tour cemented Bruce's reputation as a rock 'n' roll performer, and *The River,* released in 1980, included an actual hit single, "Hungry Heart," which brought him to the center of the pop music mainstream. The solo acoustic *Nebraska* explored the depths of his emotional headwaters in 1982, and the lyrically withering but sonically pop-friendly *Born in the USA,* released in 1984, tucked his burgeoning social consciousness in a wrapper shiny enough to propel him to unimagined heights. By the end of the decade he was one of the most popular and admired rock stars on the planet. As golden as a golden boy could ever get. But even that kind of noise, the cheering, the chiming cash registers, the admiration of critics, fans, kings, and presidents, still didn't fill the silences that had haunted him since he was a boy. He'd get there, but it would take time.

Photograph © Eric Meola

Epilogue

By the time Bruce and I sat for our birthday chat in his beach house in 2024, he had, over the years, performed "Jungleland" close to 650 times. Not nearly as many times as, say, "Born to Run" itself, which he's played more than 1,800 times and counting, but three times as often as "Night," which has been aired 264 times since 1975, according to the Brucebase website. "Jungleland" had been in the set for only two other shows on the 2023–2024 world tour, and both were in 2023. But when Bruce got to Asbury Park in mid-September 2024, he was in a different state of mind.

With so much of the set list focused on his earliest, Asbury-defined songs, it was only a little surprising to hear Bittan playing the opening chords to "Meeting Across the River," a song Bruce rarely performs even when he's digging into his past. And when that was over it was almost impossible not to anticipate the opening notes of the song that followed it on *Born to Run*, "Jungleland." Bruce looked exhilarated to be singing it, and he and the band delivered a note-perfect performance, from Bittan's piano introduction to Jake Clemons's re-creation of his uncle Clarence's famous saxophone solo. Bruce shed his Telecaster during the instrumental section and stood unadorned at the microphone for the song's finale, tracking the Magic Rat from his respite with the barefoot girl into the tunnel where he falls, gunned down, in Bruce's words, by his own dream. He went through the rest, the ambulance picking up the body, the bystanders looking the other way, the poets struck dumb by the darkness of what they'd witnessed. Then he unleashed the howls, still a spellbinding moment after all these years. Bruce kept one hand on the microphone, the other gripping the mic stand as he dug for breath, but as he got to the final howl, the one that reaches up before it settles down into the resolving note, thereby tracing the conclusion of the Rat's short, tragic life, he stretched his arms to their full length, lifting his hands to shoulder height, holding them aloft for a long moment in the manner of Christ on the cross.

At the post-concert party in the Wonder Bar a couple of hours later, Bruce enthused about the show and was particularly happy about the performance of "Jungleland." He'd been looking forward to that one, it always felt more special when he did it in New Jersey. And since he'd written the thing in that house just a few miles north of where he was playing, well, yeah. He was gobbling a cheeseburger and fries, waving to friends, not in a moment when he was prepared to talk about deeper matters. But when I asked him about that Christly move he'd made at the end of the song, assuming the cruciform position during the final howl of "Jungleland," he looked puzzled. "Huh," he said. "I don't think I was even aware I was doing that."

On his birthday a week later, Bruce is more forthcoming, at least when it comes to acknowledging the religious currents in *Born to Run*. Was Landau correct, I ask him, in his tracing of the album's story—from the appearance of a woman named Mary at its start to the Magic Rat's crucifixion in its final moments—to the story of Jesus? This time around he simply shrugs. "That's it," he says. "That's about right."

Time has passed. The logs in the fireplace have burned to embers, the tequila is down to a final sip at the bottom of the glass. There's plenty more where that came from, but outside the maritime fog is thinning, the sun just coming through. It's fun to reminisce but there's still plenty of daylight ahead of us and when that's gone, well, as Bruce once wrote and has sung again and again in theaters, arenas, stadiums, and every other kind of venue over the last fifty years, there's magic in the night.

Earlier that summer I spent the better part of a week in a recording studio in midtown Manhattan listening to tapes of the *Born to Run* recording sessions. The facility on West Forty-Third Street is now called Battery Studios, but between 1968 and 1987 it was the site of the Record Plant. I was hearing the original *Born to Run* tapes in the same recording studio where the vast majority of the album had been made. Most of the original equipment had been replaced, probably multiple times in the ensuing decades, swept away by tide after tide of technological advancement. But there's a spirit power in these places and when I went down the hall to grab some water or use the bathroom I'd think about the months Bruce had spent there in 1975, summoning *Born to Run* into being. I was twelve years old when I first heard the title song on a car radio coming home from a Boy Scout hike in the fall of 1975, and though I wasn't sure what to make of it at first I caught up soon enough, and by the time I was a sophomore in high school I'd spend hours alone in the living room of my family's house, headphones clamped over my ears and *Born to Run* going full blast. The songs seemed perfect to me, each note in place, each word and exclamation coming at exactly the right moment, in exactly the right way. I have a vivid memory of a winter evening when I was about fifteen or sixteen, way out in the horse latitudes of adolescence, so lost and lonely and bereft of hope that nothing could touch me. Then I put on *Born to Run* and though my teenage despair deafened me to the first three minutes and fifty seconds of "Thunder Road," that line about the town full of losers broke through. Max Weinberg hit the drums and then it was that coda, that plainspoken yet somehow heroic melody ringing out over those three chords, that brought me back. That made me believe that something was waiting for me in the world. And that even if it was off somewhere in the distance, and even if the journey would seem impossibly rough at times, I had to look for it. And the road ran right outside my door.

I'm sorry if it sounds corny, or like typical middle-aged-white-guy bullshit, but that's what happened to me. The music felt supernatural that night, and I've felt myself being drawn into the same spell countless times while listening to *Born to Run* since then. I have long since gotten over the idea that a pop song, or any artistic creation, comes into existence through magic. Every work of art is the product of someone's extraordinary effort. But some projects still feel surrounded by at least some measure of grace. So as our conversation begins to tail off I ask Bruce if *Born to Run* ever felt that way, even fleetingly. He holds his glass in front of his face for a moment, takes a sip, and shakes his head. "I lived through it, right? So I have too much experience of it to feel like it was magical." And even now the emotional tempest he suffered through along the way, due in large part to his own emotional reflexes, shadows his feelings about the music. "You know, it was a very intense period of work. Figuring out what I wanted to write about, how I wanted to write about it, learning how I wanted to make my record sound."

Something else was obviously going on, too.

"It was a very intense period of self-discovery, a very intense period of identifying myself and finding my identity and who I wanted to be."

Now we're finishing up. Bruce jabs at the remnants of his fire. I pack my recorders and notebooks into my bag, and he walks me back outside to where my rental car sits in the driveway. Asbury

Park is off in the north, Long Branch just a few miles beyond there. He points out a few places I might want to visit, connecting the dots between where we're standing and where he used to live, where the band used to rehearse, where he was scribbling in his notebook when this or that came to him.

I've had a few chances to ask Bruce about his work over the years and he often likes to minimize his emotional connection to particular songs or events. It's easy to understand why. If everyone else in the world has spent the last fifty years romanticizing your work, how could you possibly be interested in doing it for yourself? Sometimes I'll ask him about this-or-that song, or the point in such-and-such a show when he said or did this legendary thing. What was he thinking? How did it feel? He'll shoot me a look like he's not sure which of our heads he wants to smash against a brick wall first.

So, after all our conversation about *Born to Run,* I don't bother asking if he thinks about the record every August 25, the anniversary of its release. Instead, he just starts talking about it on his own. He isn't even looking at me then, just kind of gazing over my shoulder, entertaining a memory.

"I'm very, very fond of it," he says. "And on its anniversaries, I get in a car and I play it from start to finish, right? I just drive around listening. And I always make sure I end up in Long Branch, at West End Court, where I wrote it. I get there right before the end, right before 'Jungleland.' And I park there. I sit by the curb and I let 'Jungleland' play, all the way through, while I sit outside the little house I wrote it in."

Acknowledgments

The idea for this book came to me in the spring of 2024, which meant I had to report and write the whole thing within a few months, the rhythms of modern publishing being what they are. I had a bit of a head start, due to the work I did on *Bruce,* the biography I published in 2012, but covering the entire expanse of Bruce's life and career hadn't allowed for the sort of close attention to any particular album that this project required. So there was still a lot to learn, and quite a bit of new information to chase down and digest. Doing this required the cooperation, help, and patience of many people.

My first thanks go to Bruce Springsteen and Jon Landau, both of whom were generous with their time, encouragement, and memories. Thanks also to Mike Appel, Bruce's original manager and coproducer, whose contributions to the first three albums, and to building Bruce's recording career from the ground up, cannot be overstated.

Many thanks to the members of the E Street Band who played on the *Born to Run* sessions. All of the surviving members took the time to share their memories of the making of the album, along with the early years of their band's career and the long, slow slog from the Student Prince in Asbury Park to the heights of *Billboard*'s national charts: Roy Bittan, Clarence Clemons (whom I interviewed in 2011, just a few months before he passed away), Vini Lopez (an essential source as I was getting to know the Asbury Park and E Street music scenes in 2010–2012), David Sancious, Garry Tallent, Steven Van Zandt, and Max Weinberg, all of whom shared their time and insights into music, the music business, and the culture they were navigating in the early and mid-1970s. Thanks also to Randy Brecker, who left a big imprint on *Born to Run*, even if he was only in the studio for a single evening.

Also generous with their time and memories: studio engineers Jimmy Iovine, Thom Panunzio, and Louis Lahav, all of whom have gone on to big careers with other partners and in other contexts.

At Sony/Columbia: Al Teller, Ron Oberman, Glen Brunman, Paul Rappaport, Michael Pillot, Peter Philbin, Ron McCarrell, Matthew Kelly, Greg Linn, Timothy Smith, Rob Santos. I'd also like to give posthumous thanks to the Columbia executives who passed away after they shared their memories when I was working on the biography: Walter Yetnikoff, Bruce Lundvall, and Steve Popovich.

Even more thanks for the memories and insights of E Street staffers, friends, and fellow travelers: Stephen Appel, Mike Batlan, Sam McKeith, Bob Spitz, Rick Seguso, Albee Tellone, Peter Golden, and James Segelstein.

I spoke in depth with members of the extended Springsteen family during the writing of the biography in 2009–2012, and I returned to those interviews often this time around. Many thanks to the wonderful Adele Springsteen (RIP), Virginia Springsteen Shave, Pamela Springsteen, Dora Kirby (RIP), Eda Urbelis (RIP), and Glenn Cashion. I also had the benefit of the experiences and insights of George Theiss (RIP) and Bobby Duncan.

I leaned on the work, thoughts, and generosity of the writers who preceded me writing about Bruce and his work. Most particularly Dave Marsh, Maureen Orth, Jay Cocks, J. Garrett Andrews, and Joel Zakem. And of course Charles R. Cross, whose brains, wit, and friendship I will always miss.

For his knowledge of Freehold's history and the Springsteen family's legacy, and for his friendship and excellent counsel: Kevin Coyne.

The filmmaker Barry Rebo is responsible for virtually all of the '70s-era archival footage of Bruce and his band, from numerous early shows (including two complete shows from the Bottom Line stand in August 1975) to the incredible footage of the early "Jungleland" sessions in January 1975. I've been able to see the majority of this work, twice over in some cases, and can only say that it's a miracle it exists. There are quite a few heroes in this story, and Barry is one to whom we all owe a debt of gratitude. I can't thank him enough for his help.

You could say the same about the photographer Eric Meola, whose iconic photographs of Bruce and company can be seen on the cover of *Born to Run* and throughout this book.

I owe so much to my friends at Doubleday: my editor, Jason Kaufman, plus his colleagues Lily Dondoshansky and Elena Hershey. Thanks also to Corinne Cummings, for her authoritative fact-checking.

At Writers House: Dan Conaway, agent extraordinaire; Sydnee Harlan; and Sofia Bolido.

Claire Dederer is my partner in life, love, and dog walking, but wait, there's more: she lived this entire project with me, accompanied me to shows in three cities and two countries, and went over every word of the manuscript with me in all their iterations. She made this book significantly better than it would have been without her help.

My kids are an endless source of joy, support, and inspiration: Abe, Teddy, and Max. And now also my stepkids: Lou and Ash Barcott.

For my final thanks I should return to Bruce Springsteen, whose willingness to consider his entire self, including his flaws and failures, is just as inspiring as his artistry. He is, after everything else, a good guy.

Bibliography

Cross, Charles, and the editors of *Backstreets* magazine. *Springsteen: The Man and His Music.* New York: Harmony Books, 1989.
Germaine, Nicki. *Springsteen: Liberty Hall.* Self-published.
Hiatt, Brian. *Bruce Springsteen: The Stories Behind the Songs.* New York: Abrams, 2019.
Rolling Stone, the editors of. *Bruce Springsteen: The Rolling Stone Files.* New York: Hyperion, 1996.
Schneier, Barry. *Bruce Springsteen: Rock and Roll Future.* Chapel Hill, NC: The Backstreets Publishing Empire, Inc., 2018.
Springsteen, Bruce. *Born to Run.* New York: Simon & Schuster, 2016.
White, Ryan. *Springsteen: Album by Album.* New York: Sterling, 2014.

PERMISSIONS ACKNOWLEDGMENTS

Grateful acknowledgment is made to Sony Music Publishing (US) LLC for permission to reprint song lyrics:

"Born to Run" by Bruce Springsteen. © 1975 Sony Music Publishing (US) LLC and Eldridge Publishing Co.

"Tenth Avenue Freeze-Out" by Bruce Springsteen. © 1975 Sony Music Publishing (US) LLC and Eldridge Publishing Co.

"Thunder Road" by Bruce Springsteen. © 1975 Sony Music Publishing (US) LLC and Eldridge Publishing Co.

"Night" by Bruce Springsteen. © 1975 Sony Music Publishing (US) LLC and Eldridge Publishing Co.

"Backstreets" by Bruce Springsteen. © 1975 Sony Music Publishing (US) LLC and Eldridge Publishing Co.

"Meeting Across the River" by Bruce Springsteen. © 1975 Sony Music Publishing (US) LLC and Eldridge Publishing Co.

"Jungleland" by Bruce Springsteen. © 1975 Sony Music Publishing (US) LLC and Eldridge Publishing Co.

"The Promise" by Bruce Springsteen. © 2010 Sony Music Publishing (US) LLC and Eldridge Publishing Co.

All rights administered by Sony Music Publishing (US) LLC, 1005 17th Avenue South, Suite 800, Nashville, TN 37212. All rights reserved. Used by permission.

ABOUT THE AUTHOR

PETER AMES CARLIN is the author of several books, including *The Name of This Band Is R.E.M.*, *Sonic Boom: The Impossible Rise of Warner Bros. Records,* published in 2021, and *Bruce,* a biography of Bruce Springsteen, published in 2012. Carlin has also been a freelance journalist, a senior writer at *People* in New York City, and a television columnist and feature writer at *The Oregonian* in Portland. A regular speaker on music, writing, and popular culture, Carlin lives in Seattle.